MW01098358

Copyright © 1992 by Marian L. Swain.
All rights reserved.

No part of this book may be reproduced or used in any
form or by any means without prior written permission
of the author or publisher, excepting brief quotes used
in connection with reviews.

The quotation at the beginning of *Gilbert Said* is from
Robert A. Henning's foreword to *The Silver Years of the
Alaska Canned Salmon Industry* (Alaska Northwest
Publishing Co., 1976). Used by permission.

Printed in the United States of America
Second printing March, 1993
Hardscratch Press, Walnut Creek, California
Library of Congress Catalog Card Number: 92-072443
ISBN: 0-9625429-4-6

2 3 4 5 6 7 8 9 0

gilbert said

An oldtimer's tales of the Haida-Tlingit waterways of Alaska

Collected and with an introduction
by Marian L. Swain

A HARDSCRATCH PRESS BOOK

To my children and grandchildren,
Harlan, Scott and Sandee,
Kelly, Lacie, Matthew and Robert,
and my sister, Maleta

⋀ ⋀ ⋀

GILBERT'S STORIES were taped from conversations I had with Gilbert and Carolyn McLeod in Ketchikan and on Gilbert's boat the Keeper in 1968 and 1969, and at Warm Beach, Washington, in the 1970s. Carolyn and Gilbert read all the stories in their first draft.

My daughter-in-law, Sandee Swain, typed the stories in good form from my transcriptions and has encouraged me a great deal. Gilbert's stepdaughters, Mary Ecklund and Michele McGill, also have been helpful: Michele allowing me to use her oil portrait of Gilbert, and Mary gathering and lending family photos. Helen Brown Sanderson generously lent historic photos and Haida community documents.

I owe thanks also to Mary Smith, the librarian at Ketchikan, and to the staff of the Alaska State Historical Library at Juneau, as well as to Isabel Miller of Sitka, an oldtimer and perpetual historian. Muriel Newsome honed my skills, and Grace Cornwell always needled me to finish the project.

My family and friends have patiently seen me through the many revisions of this book. I mention in particular my late husband, Charles Zentner, Nancy and Owen Hunt, Carol Graham, Billie Anderson, and my sister, Maleta Boatman, who always encourages. Helen Young Meilleur understood my need to preserve this material and my discouragement that the project was going so slowly. She shared family material about the Youngs.

Special thanks go to Bob Pickrell, publisher and editor of the *New Alaskan,* for his interest and enthusiasm. Several of Gilbert's stories have appeared in the *New Alaskan,* and seeing them in print encouraged me to continue. Finally, thanks to Jackie Pels, David Johnson and John Boring, who have made *Gilbert Said* a reality.

This book is for Carolyn.

Remains of a communal house, about 1900 (Winter & Pond, courtesy of Alaska Historical Library, 87-1350)

For those who did not know these times now past,
all we can say is, "This was a time.
Those were the days we will never forget.
You should have been there."
                                        —*Robert A. Henning*

GILBERT McCLEOD'S mother and father arrived in the Haida village of Howkan at the southeasternmost tip of Alaska in 1882 and 1883. She taught school in Chief Skulka's best house on the waterfront. His father helped construct the sawmill on Dall Island and there sawed wood for the building of the Presbyterian mission.

As we came out of Craig in 1969 on Gilbert's 33-foot boat, the Keeper, on our way to Hydaburg, Gilbert said, "See that island starboard? That's San Juan Bautista. We used to go deer hunting there. And portside, that island is Brokey Joe's. During Prohibition days, Brokey Joe had a still, making hoochinoo. Long before that, Thomas Skulka, chief of Howkan, stopped on the beach overnight on his way to Fish Egg Island and had quite an adventure there."

That was how the trip started, and it continued in the same manner, with Gilbert regaling me with tales from his life.

That year, 1969, was the year I met Gilbert. His wife, Carolyn, had invited me to their apartment for the evening. Although I'd lived in Ketchikan 15 years, I was a cheechako, an outsider. But I was a respectful observer and listener, and Carolyn encouraged Gilbert to share his stories with me. She was proud of his heritage, and she helped others understand this man who never learned to drive a car but knew the inside waters of southeastern Alaska as an Iowa farmer knows his back roads.

Gilbert was born July 19, 1904, at Big Daykoo, now called

McLeod Bay after his father. Raised as he was among the Haida, it was to be expected he would marry a girl of one of the west coast villages. From Nettie Nix, his first wife, he learned more about old, old Alaska. With Nettie he had nine children: Maggie and Ray, now of California; Jean, who lives in Texas; Nettie of Alaska; and Dick, Molly, Addie, Skip and Della of Washington.

As the children arrived, Gilbert struggled to support them with his salmon and herring fishing, seining, trap pirating and Noyes Island cannery work. Sometimes in the winter he hired on as crew on mail boats.

"We had no fathometer, no radar," he recalled. "Just a few navigational aids—that was all. We had a sounding lead and seldom used it."

He first had a little troller, the Peggy; next, the Delaware, a schooner type. The Jadah, the luckiest boat he ever had, was a 42-foot purse seiner. (Jadah means "girl" in the Haida language.) The Yellowstone, a 45-foot former halibut boat, he used both as a fish packer and as a charter boat. The Harvester was a large purse seiner of a different style than the others; the Spage, a 30-foot double-ender.

When I met him and his second wife, Carolyn, they owned the Keeper, on which we went to Hydaburg. They wanted to show me firsthand some of the west coast waters and to introduce me to Hydaburg people from Howkan.

Gilbert had married Carolyn Petterson MacIssaac in 1959. She had two daughters, Mary Ecklund of Ketchikan and Michele McGill of Camano Island, Washington.

Carolyn was an Alaskan oldtimer, too, the daughter of Peter A. ("Good-Lookin'") Petterson, who fished all the waters of Alaska. The Natives called him "Pete Calugen"—Calugen meant good-looking. Carolyn lived in Seattle as a child, but she went to high school in Ketchikan and years ago worked for the Tongass Trading Co. there. Eventually she owned Carolyn's Clothing Store in Ketchikan. After her retirement in January 1969, she and Gilbert moved to Warm Beach, Washington, but they continued to spend the summers on the waters of Southeast Alaska until her death in 1985.

Gilbert's stories don't sound the same without Carolyn's appreciative laughter. Neither are they the same in print without his Haida-Tlingit cadence. But Carolyn and I agreed that they are too valuable a record of the people and the folklore of southeastern Alaska to be lost. Carolyn died June 28, 1985. Gilbert is now living at the Pioneer Home in Ketchikan. I am 77, and it is time for this book.

ᐱ ᐱ ᐱ

Gilbert's parents were Clara Amy Gould McLeod and William Donald McLeod. It was to Howkan (sometimes spelled Howcan) that his mother, age 18, youngest of many siblings, had come in 1882 from Buckhannon, West Virginia, to be "Teacher," a title she kept all of her life. She was joining her brother, Captain H. Loomis Gould, a missionary who had come earlier the same year

Members of the Christian Endeavor Society, Howkan (courtesy of Helen Brown Sanderson)

with his wife, Rebecca Reed Gould, and their two children, Hal and Vesta.

In Howkan, Clara taught first in Chief Skulka's best house on the crescent-shaped waterfront. Skulka's house proudly displayed a flagpole with the U.S. flag, a bell tower with a large bell, and a sign in English saying "House of the World." A large gray stone guarded the beach, and totems stood at the front of Skulka's house and many of the others. In front of the chief's house, a totem with a "Boston man" on the top depicted the kidnapping of the daughter of a famous woman of the Eagle clan by the Boston men, as the early Yankee sailors were called. In front of the Yeltatzie family's house next door, a totem displayed the two-finned whale.

In the fall of 1882, a sawmill was sent to Howkan, a gift of a Brooklyn, New York, missionary society. William Donald McLeod, who was to become Gilbert's father 21 years later, arrived in the spring of 1883. He was a short, stocky, 30-year-old New York ex-serviceman of Scottish heritage, a jack-of-all-trades, including sawyer, machinist and carpenter. With the help of the village men, he assembled the sawmill near a good water supply on Dall Island across from Howkan and sawed wood to build the mission buildings and houses for the villagers.

Clara's brother, Captain Gould, felt that Howkan could become a model village with the school, mission buildings, homes and a Christian storekeeper. James Wright Young, a lay missionary, had been sent to work at the Presbyterian school and children's home in Wrangell. He was transferred to Howkan with his bride, who had been a housekeeper at the children's home. They operated the store. A few years later, Young also carried the mail.

The little village might have become schizophrenic with the name changes it endured. On July 24, 1881, it was established as "Jackson," but according to early traveler and writer E. Ruhannah Scidmore, the U.S. Post Office recognized it as the "Haida mission" rather than Jackson. On May 15, 1886, it was designated "Howcan" and on April 11, 1890, Jackson again, until it was

Howkan, about 1897 (Winter & Pond, courtesy of Alaska Historical Library, 87-50)

changed back to Howcan on May 16, 1903. On January 31, 1917, it was discontinued as a post office. By then all the families had moved away.

In 1885, Congress appropriated money for public schools for Alaskans. The U.S. government appointed Dr. Sheldon Jackson general agent of education for Alaska. The missionary school, no longer in Skulka's house, became the public school. By 1887, Gilbert's mother had the teaching commission for the town at a salary of $600 a year.

She taught there for 13 consecutive years and then again later for two more years. She had a great influence on the lives of the people. When she died in Craig in the 1930s, those friends who had called her "Teacher" all her life helped Gilbert with the expense of her funeral so she could have the cement-lined grave they knew she wanted.

Sheldon Jackson reported in 1886 that the temporary shelter then used as a school had been crushed by a heavy snowstorm.

The teacher had sent good monthly reports, Jackson noted. The Haida were considered the best people on the north Pacific coast, he said, and he urged that immediate steps be taken to erect a schoolhouse suitable for this important Haida center.

The number of Clara Gould's students varied each month, but she taught 81 to 123 students of all ages per year. Families moved in from various camps and houses and then moved again each spring to begin their gathering and harvesting. Dr. Jackson and the 1890 census taker were uniform in praise of the continued "excellent teaching staff," namely Clara Amy Gould.

On February 27, 1891, Clara Gould married William McLeod. After their marriage they both worked part-time at the village store. Gilbert would say, "This was when my folks had the store," or, "My mother told me about taking furs on the ships to Victoria for trading." Gilbert's older sister was born at this time. She is now Margaret Wood of Lynwood, Washington. The McLeods also had a foster son, George Hamilton, who lived his adult years and died in Craig.

In 1897, the McLeods went from Howkan to a gold claim they had staked at Big Daykoo, where Gilbert was born, and they lived there until 1911, when Gilbert was 7. Big Daykoo is in Kaigani Haida country. At the head of Big Daykoo, on the southwestern bank where a sign reading "Cable Crossing" now stands, William McLeod built a plank house. He laid out a fenced-in vegetable and flower garden on each side of the walk to the high-water mark. Behind the house, he worked some of his numerous mineral claims in tortuous endeavors, digging hundreds of feet of tunnels into a hillside that was a slide area. Gilbert's recollection was that his father was lode mining.

Mining historian John Bufvers notes that developing the McLeod Bay prospect was expensive. William McLeod apparently found some schist of good value, but the grade would not permit mining on a large scale. Bufvers mentions also a rich outcrop discovered by William McLeod on the beach near the shore of Sukkwan Island. Although too much powder was used and much gold was blasted into the water, McLeod probably recovered a few thousand dollars, Bufvers says.

In the midst of these struggles, Clara McLeod became a storied cook.

Gilbert's favorite foods are still the Haida red potato and salmon, but his mother also dried seaweed and halibut and made kelp pickles and fresh berry jams. Because it produced a steady fire and burned for a long time, she baked with spruce-wood heat, using potato water with the yeast for bread. George Hamilton, Gilbert's foster brother, provided wild game for the table and taught Margaret, Gilbert's older sister, to shoot and hunt. The family had a milk cow called Jessie and a dog, Bruiser. They had bone china and Willow Ware from Victoria, B.C., and William McLeod made beautiful yellow cedar rocking chairs.

Into this home Gilbert was born. One of the respected members of the old Haida people—Lucinda Westcott's brother and Helen Sanderson's grand-uncle—said the new baby must be an Yeltatzie, born as he was in Kaigani country. His parents named him Gilbert, a family name of the Goulds, and Donald for his father. A second daughter, Jean, died many years ago in Matanuska, north of Anchorage.

With all her family responsibilities, Clara McLeod still visited camps with her little organ and led services. Gilbert's sister Margaret said, "Although Mother could not carry a tune and had little to sing about, she was always singing. Her favorite was 'Work for the Night Is Coming.'" From Saturday night at dusk until Sunday evening at sunset in their religious household, they didn't even pack in a stick of wood. Kindling was all in the house on Saturday. Sunday was a day of rest—except for Clara McLeod, who cooked breakfast, a dinner about three and a light supper.

When they decided to leave the bay, William McLeod was offered $10,000 for the property, but he thought the place was worth more and so recovered nothing. The family returned to Howkan, where they lived on the beach in a large two-story house. A man named James Rowan shared some of the mining claims, and some ill will followed the partnership because nothing was recouped.

At this time, people from all the Haida villages, including Howkan, were being encouraged by the government to move to Hydaburg in order to consolidate services such as schools. Some, including the Yeltatzies, the Bells, the Skulkas and the Morrisons, did not want to leave their homes. W.E. Ross ("Howkan Ross"), who was then the storekeeper, prevailed on the U.S. commissioner to keep the school at Howkan open a few more years and persuaded Clara McLeod to teach.

This was Gilbert's first association with children outside his own family, and he felt strange as a minority in the Haida village. He had heard Chinook from visitors to the mining camp but had not heard a great deal of the Haida language. He found the village scary. There was a graveyard on the spit and more graves in

Lay minister John Brown's house, built in 1908 at Klinquan, where he was preaching, then disassembled and moved on rafts, first to Howkan and finally to Hydaburg, in 1916 (courtesy of Helen Brown Sanderson)

We, the undersigned, Alaskan Natives of Hydaburg, Alaska, hereby
declare that we have given up our old tribal relationships; that we recog
nize no chief of clan or tribal family; that we have given up all claim t
or interest in tribal and communal houses; that we live in one family km
houses in accordance with the customs of civilization; that we observe the
marriage laws of the United States; that our children take the name of the
father and belong equally to the father and mother, and that the rights of
the maternal uncle to direct the children are no longer recognized and
that in the case of the death of either parent we recognize the laws of the
United States relative to inheritance of property; that we have discarded
the totem and recognize the Stars and Stripes as our only emblem; and that
we are a self-supporting and law abiding people.

We therefore believe that we have fulfilled all requirements
necessary to citizenship in the United States, and we respectfully request
the Congress of the United States to pass a law granting to us the full ri
rights of citizenship.

Names:	Names:
Paul D Morrison	J S Brown
George Haldane	Luke Frank
Thaddeus Isaac	Charles Stast
James George	Matthew Charles
Paul S cowl	Thomas S cowl
Rufus Edenshaw	Albert Nathang
Henry Boyan	James Cedens
Wm George	Alex Reel
Mason Frank	John Wallace
Edwin Scott	Alex H. Slavis
Richard Klunaket	Fred Grant
Hugh Toga	Joseph Klunaker
George Hamilton	Peter Pathtan
John Pathtan	George Vandel

the village, which held boarded-up houses with empty spaces between.

One of his bright memories is of Jones Yeltatzie, who made him models of the MV Alf and the Forrester, modern cannery tenders for those days. He used shoelace eyes from old shoes for portholes. Jones' father was a canoe builder, said to be so rich that he started his fires with ulokan grease. The elder Yeltatzie worked on the beach constructing a 10-fathom red cedar canoe.

In school, "Teacher" thwacked the kids on the head for speaking Haida. Gilbert pulled the braids of the girls. He tells few stories of this time in his life.

In the summers of 1913 and 1914, the family went to a large handtrolling camp on the bird refuge on Forrester Island, 14½ miles from Dall Island. Gilbert's mother had been sending bread out with the packers, the J.T. Todd and the Admiral Dewey, to be sold to the handtrollers, whose home base was the Alaska Fish Co., the cannery at what was to become Waterfall, on Prince of Wales Island. With a $10 special-use permit from the Department of Agriculture, Clara McLeod set up a bakery on Forrester Island. A packer moved the big iron cookstove, tents and other gear from Howkan.

Young Gilbert watched the handtrollers lining up to put their boats in the water, then at the end of the day bobbing in the water vying for their turn to come ashore. The buyer strutted around camp with a sack of gold coins to pay for the fish.

The handtrollers came from all walks of life, ex-prizefighters, bankers, sailors, a world champion bicycle rider. All were "water gypsies of the Pacific," says Charles Lillard, quoting a 1911 author. They spun yarns for the boy of 9 or 10 who wandered the camp during the daytime hours and slept the summer nights on a mattress put together of hemlock brush to keep out the shrews.

From Howkan the family moved to Sulzer, the hub for copper mining. Clara McLeod cooked at the hotel and took in roomers at home. From those days Gilbert had many stories about people such as likable Charley Sulzer, who bought the Jumbo Mine from

Aaron Shellhouse. Sulzer was a political rival of Judge James Wickersham. There were tall Texan Rastus Brown, who had hitched a ride from Nome on the sloop the Sea Wolf, and the hapless mail carrier who hauled the mail over the portage 3½ miles on the corduroy road from Cholmondeley Sound to the head of Portage Bay. And Harry Brice, playing "Are You From Dixie?" on the piano at Coppermount. Gilbert remembered learning to run Charley Sulzer's boat, the Lydia, with Bert Davey. In 1916, when he was 12, Gilbert worked at the Rose Inlet Cannery and later told a couple of stories of murder among the gambling crew.

The McLeods eventually moved to Craig, named for Craig Millar, who with George Hamilton had started a mild-cure station there. Several of the Howkan families went there and to Ketchikan in preference to moving to Hydaburg.

Gilbert told of it all—of handtrolling and traps, web stations and canneries . . .

Of Thunderbird, Raven and Shag . . .

Of mailboats and smugglers . . .

Of pit lighting and deadfall traps . . .

Of Brokey Joe, John Landerman, Hank Adams, Rastus Brown and Pike Pole Slim . . .

Of Lydia Charles and Cora Mueller . . .

Of Luke Frank, Captain Edenso and Dewey Stack . . .

And yes, even of John Barrymore.

Gilbert gave me this poem of his in the 1960s, before environmental protection was a popular notion. He was ahead of his time.

> They say the Indian's wasteful.
> Many times you've heard it told.
> But there's nothing near so wasteful
> As the white man's greed for gold.

They have ruined all the fisheries.
Now they've started in on logs.
They're rooting up the salmon streams
Just like a bunch of hogs.

They are the world's greatest sportsmen.
They shoot bucks, does and fawns.
They dive and cut loose tons of kelp
When it's full of herring spawn.

With ready cash they come to town,
They say to have a ball.
In bars they brag about their deeds,
Half full of alcohol.

But now, my friends, if things don't change,
Nature's gift will soon be gone.
And we will have no little fish
For they'll have no place to spawn.

GILBERT'S WORLD lies in the southern half of the
Alexander Archipelago. In 1867, the year the United
States purchased Alaska from Russia, this panhandle
was named for a Russian czar. The archipelago is about
300 miles north and south and 60 miles wide.
It has more than 1,100
islands charted, and
there may be more.
Gilbert's life began
on the shore of
Big Daykoo on
Dall Island, at Cape
Muzon, the south-
eastern tip of
Alaska. On Dall Island's west coast lies
the Pacific Ocean, on its east coast Kaigani
Strait. (The Haida word kaigani means strait.) Dixon
Entrance, off Dall Island's southern tip, separates it from
Canada's Queen Charlotte Islands, from whence came
the Haida families to settle as far north as the Tlingit
Hannega country of Klawock, building their villages on
the west coasts of the islands to take advantage of the
afternoon sun. Lush cedar, hemlock and spruce forests,
heavy undergrowth and mushy muskeg with Paul
Bunyan–size skunk cabbage and ferns cover the land
to the shorelines.

Nome

ALASKA

CANADA

0 Miles 200

Bering
Sea

Fairbanks

Mt. McKinley

Anchorage

Juneau

Portland Canal

Gulf of
Alaska

Alexander
Archipelago

GILBERT'S WORLD

QUEEN
CHARLOTTE
ISLANDS
(CANADA)

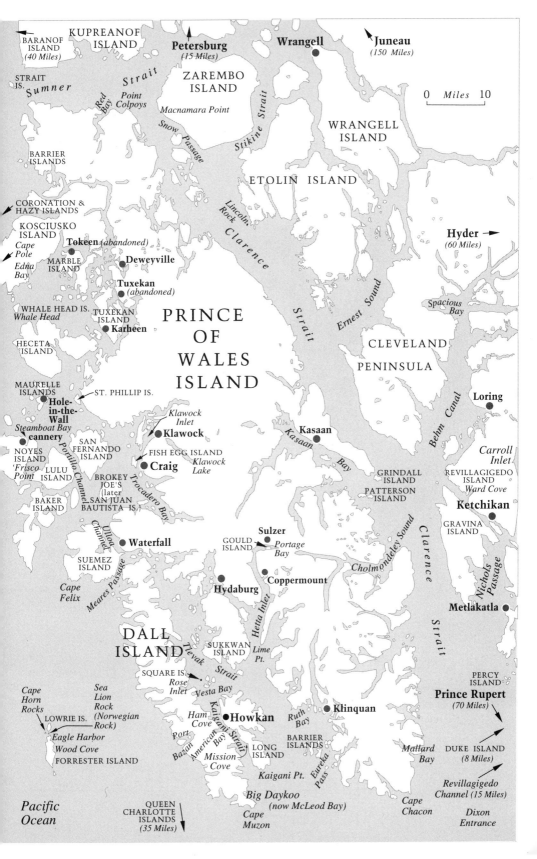

Chapter I. Gilbert in 1969
Talked About the Haida

How MANY of those who talk about the Haida of my mother's day and before really knew the Haida?

Do you know the Haida were great traders? They traded the potatoes and turnips they raised; they trapped and hunted and traded mink, bear, beaver and sea otter pelts. In March, when the Nass River Tsimpseans from Port Chester came to them with ulokan —eulachon or candlefish grease—the Haida put it up in their cedar boxes and took it as far north as the Chilkat to trade. It brought good prices in furs.

Each family had a business of some kind. Some families were the hunters and some were the trappers; some families were the canoe makers and some were the silver carvers.

Because of the craftsmanship, their red cedar canoes were the most desired on the west coast. Red cedar is available only in Haida country. North of Point Baker there is no more. Red cedar is light and bends easily. The canoes were 40 to 60 feet long, and the largest of them were capable of carrying 30 to 40 persons. Because the bow and stern projected "righters" two to three feet beyond the canoe, they were unsinkable. When capsized they righted themselves and when filled with water wouldn't sink below the surface of the ocean. They were a beautiful craft.

Every spring the family brought in a good red cedar log and pulled it up on the beach. The canoe maker worked at it all summer, hewing out the log and preparing it, steaming it into shape with hot rocks.

Another thing about the Haida. They had a season for everything. They were enterprising. In the spring they knew what time everything was ready to gather to eat. They'd go get seaweed and they'd dry it. They dried halibut; they dried venison. Then they went after bird eggs and herring eggs. Old Walter Ketah from Klawock was the best bird egg gatherer around. Each thing as it was, in season. They planted their gardens of potatoes and turnips. When the fur got prime, they went trapping.

Then the canneries were starting, and before that the salteries. They employed a few people and used the fishermen, too. And that way of life, the salteries and canneries, did not interfere that much with the Haida system. They participated in it and profited by it.

Then all that went out. That's the reason the Haida became hard up. And the worst of it all was that it was shameful to be poor—and hurtful to the whole family.

They all respected success.

⋀ ⋀ ⋀

It's a long story about why those early Alaskans had so many houses and camps. A man and his entire family might trap on Gravina Island across from Ketchikan, taking what they needed for themselves. However, if any signs showed up that the survival of the species was threatened, the trappers would leave. The next season they'd camp someplace else. This was the procedure with fish and all wildlife, until the traders and the fishermen came. So the Alaskans had many camps and houses. In this limitless lush country there were abundant sites for them.

They protected all of nature—for example, the young mergansers. When I was a kid, lots of these small birds that half fly and half run skittered across the water. Any kid naturally wanted to chase them. The old people just had a fit. "Bad luck's going to happen to you when you hurt something like that," they said.

Newcomers in Ketchikan in the '60s used coots along the waterfront for target practice.

26

The oldtime Alaskan, Haida or Tlingit, would never have done that—kill just to be killing. They were strict with their laws about behavior. They lived up to their laws.

They had strict rules about how they were to behave and how they were to be disciplined. The men meted out justice surely and swiftly. You bet your life. Those punished by other men of their own clan were no good.

They had strict rules about whom they were supposed to marry.

They had strict rules about slaves.

They had strict rules about all family behavior. The difference is, they followed their laws or social customs.

For example: A high-toned Haida didn't talk much.

A person always had to repay a favor.

A son-in-law never spoke to his mother-in-law.

Raven Cons the Shag

A common scene in Howkan in the olden days:
In the early evening the ravens on the beach called a constant "kla wock, kla wock," then circled up to the east to tall hemlock trees where the large birds had their nests. Seagulls squabbled among themselves and were annoyed their beach was disturbed. Out on a floating limb sat a cormorant, drying off.

(I've heard both Haida and Tlingit oldtimers tell stories about the ravens. I can't remember from whom specifically I got my stories.)

The cormorant or shag with its graceful long neck seldom makes any noise. I think he looks dumb, and he really isn't very smart.

This is a story about one time when Raven conned Shag. Raven knew Shag was the best of fishermen, with his short, powerful legs and webbed paddle-like feet and grooved jaws.

Raven propositioned Shag: "Let's you and I go partners. You'll

27

catch the fish and I'll sell them."

Shag wasn't sure that was such a good deal. Raven explained again. Shag agreed.

He dived down, 'way far underneath the school of fish, and then up he came with a nice big one and threw it on the beach.

Raven praised Shag. "That's a dandy. Get another?" No sooner was Shag under the water than Raven ate the fish.

Shag brought up another and another—four or five more.

Raven ate them and then went to sleep. Shag came up with still another one and looked around. "Well, where are they?"

Raven hesitated. Then he said, "I'll tell you the truth. I had to taste them before I could sell them, and they were so good I just ate them. But you'll get more."

Shag was sitting there feeling really bad for himself and serious and quiet. After a spell of fishing he still sits on a floating object, either with his wings spread out drying, spread-eagled I call it, or he sits straight and tall and still.

Well, Shag has a topknot or double crest on his head. Raven said, "Look, you're lousy." He grabbed Shag by the topknot. It was a great shame to be lousy. "I got it—the louse. Here, I'll give it to you." Raven knew that with Shag's teeth, like a saw with the long narrow lateral grooves, he could crunch a louse. Raven commanded, "Crunch the louse." Shag opened his mouth for the louse, and Raven reached in with his sharp heavy beak and clipped Shag's tongue off short. And that's why to this day Shag can't make much noise.

ᐱ ᐱ ᐱ

The Alaskans lived close to the natural world. They interpreted its phenomena in their stories. Undoubtedly they noticed that Shag wasn't noisy like the seagulls, ravens and heron.

Ravens are smart. One time, anchored at old Mission Cove, Howkan, I heard fur seal barking. Raven sat on top of a hemlock and imitated the sound, with the same rhythm and pitch.

Raven and the Tide

There was a powerful old man who lived close to Kootznahoo Inlet and Head. Kootznahoo Inlet is near the Tlingit village of Angoon, on the eastern shore of Chatham Strait, northward of Killisnoo Island. With his back to the sea and to a small spit of land where he could have a steady fire at his back, the old man sat with knees pulled up, holding in the tide. He was the tidekeeper for the whole world.

Raven was living off what he could scavenge from the beach.

However, because of the way the old man was holding the water in, there wasn't much beach. Raven got tired of this, and he scolded. He watched and cawed at the diving ducks like the golden-eyes and scoters and the grebes, and he'd bomb them for minutes at a time. One of the diving ducks came up with a green sea urchin all covered with spikes. Just out of sight of the old man, with one charge over and down to the duck, Raven took the sea urchin from the duck's bill.

Then Raven started circling the old man, who asked, "What are you doing here?"

Translated into English, Raven said, "I want to warm by your fire. I'm cold. I ate too many sea urchins."

"You feathered so-and-so. You couldn't be eating sea urchins. You can't dive," grumbled the old man.

Raven scolded, "The hell I can't," and he slapped the old man on his bare back with the sea urchin and down went the old man's feet.

Out went the tide. Swoosh! Raven got busy. From the edge of the ledge, bare at low tide, Raven leaned over into the water. He grabbed fish. Halibut was too big to drag up. Raven left halibut at the edge of the ledge in deep water. The rock cod, perch and flounder Raven left in shallow water near the edge of the ledge. He liked them.

During all of this, the old man was trying to get his feet flexed again to stop the water. The force was too great, and the tide had too much velocity; so the old man could never again hold up his

29

feet to stop the tide.

The tides in Kootznahoo Inlet are surely different. The currents are swift, and in places they boil and swirl. At least at slack tide, one can get in and out of the inlet; whereas before, when the old man was sitting there, one couldn't get in and out at all.

About Raven and the Water
Running Down the Hazy Island Rocks
Off Coronation Island in Chatham Strait

Old Raven was getting pretty dry. He thought he would bring water for himself and the people. He'd have to outfox Eagle, who lived in the islands and covered the water hole. Raven stopped in Tuxekan. There he picked up some dirt, feces from a dog, and put it under his wing.

He flew on out to Coronation Island and as he alighted on a rock flipped the dirt from under his wing to a spot behind the Eagle. He greeted Eagle. "How's things going?"

Eagle anwered, "Fine. Thirsty?"

"No. No. There's lots of snow," Raven retorted, staring at the dirt he'd thrown behind Eagle. "You must be getting old."

Eagle turned to see what the crafty one was looking at. Raven commented, "Yes, you must be getting old to have an accident like that when I'm here."

Eagle apologized. "What can I do to show you I didn't mean to do that while you were here?"

Raven had planned his response. "You've got lots of water. Take a bath."

The big Eagle, clumsy on land, with an old man's rolling walk, waddled off the grass mat and pulled it away from the water hole. Raven stuck his beak down and filled himself full of water.

He flew. When he got over Warren Island he started to laugh, and water spurted out. You can still see water rivulets trickling down the edge of the island.

ⵣ ⵣ ⵣ

30

I don't pretend to get these stories just right.

Lydia Charles' Haida version of the bringing of water to the people was different. Raven came to the place where a powerful man guarded the supply. Raven took a big mouthful. He squirted water into river canyons. He spit water left into a big hole in Massett in the Queen Charlotte Islands. The water never runs dry. Up north, tunnels run all over where Raven shot out the water when the "big thing" was chasing him.

Why the Haida Came to Cape Muzon

Off those Queen Charlotte Islands, in 10-fathom-long canoes with no sails, the Haida caught halibut and were using dried halibut as one of their main sources of trade with other northeast tribes. The spirit of Halibut bothered one of the men, telling him that the villagers were getting too much.

One day as the man fished in his canoe, he got a strong strike from deep down. The sun was coming up and shone on the land across Dixon Entrance, Kaigani Point (it was later called the tip of Long Island). The man hooked the fish. It towed him halfway across toward that land. The sun shone on it all the way.

Suddenly Halibut made a dive and, breaking the line, got away.

The man turned back. On shore, he told the people he'd seen a new place to go where the sun hit the land all day. It would be an ideal place to dry halibut.

Soon they started out to the shining place. A strong wind from the west divided them, and some of the people were blown east around Cape Chacon up Clarence Strait to Kasaan and some went to Kaigani Point.

The beach was wonderful for drying fish.

∧ ∧ ∧

Some of the fables were not too different from those of the Old Testament. Maybe that's why the Haida and Tlingit believed in the Christianity brought by the missionaries. You've seen the totem at Saxman, south of Ketchikan, with the sun around the Raven's head, telling of Raven's bringing light to the world. That reminds me of Genesis.

The Haida and Tlingit also had stories of floods and a few survivors who escaped the deluge by climbing a mountain. The people knew which peak.

Raven was in most legends that accounted for the physical world. For example, there is a sand beach at Suemez Island, a portage Raven made, north of Dall Island. Because his wife was moaning with each wave's rise and fall, seasick, he wanted a smooth place to drag her canoe across the island so he wouldn't have to go into the rough waters around Cape Felix, the southern point of Suemez.

Also, a columnar formation in those western islands unusual to this part was known as Raven's house.

Tales sometimes pointed out dangers. If the superstitions were believed and acted on, it often saved the people from trouble.

ᐱ ᐱ ᐱ

The Alaskans never wasted anything, including souls. Nowadays we bury a guy and send his soul up to heaven and he stays up there flying around like an angel. Man, we've got all those souls up in heaven, and it's so crowded now they'll have to do something about it. The Haida and Tlingit of old used that soul over and over again, and the spirit comes back to you if you want him or her to.

They did not like to spank a kid or do anything hurtful to one, even hurtful to his feelings, because if a relative hadn't wanted the spirit now in the child, he wouldn't have come. I guess I kind of believe that.

ᐱ ᐱ ᐱ

My mother didn't talk much to me about her early days. However, someone told me of reading a January or February 1886 Sitka paper about the fourth Christmas she was in Howkan, 1885. Chief Skulka gave a feast. Guests came in seven canoes, paddling in rhythm to their singing, and three or four prospectors from Juneau had arrived earlier. My mother and her sister-in-law, Rebecca Reed Gould, were the only non-Native women there.

The chief had hired a cook from British Columbia. Three tables 30 feet long upstairs in his house and two tables 20 feet long on the lower level were set with white tablecloths, china plates and cups, and glass fruit dishes, and waiters in white jackets served the food.

I think my mother lived for nine years with the Goulds in the parsonage near the church at the back of the village, but I think after she was married she lived near the water. Someone said she lived in a Russian house, but I don't know anything about that.

The Shaman

Carolyn told this story:

On one of our trips on the Keeper, we had my grandson Stewie along. One day we anchored in a little cove on a small island near Whale Head. While Gilbert rested, Stewie and I took the skiff and rowed ashore. We wandered through the undergrowth over fallen logs and muskeg holes.

Suddenly we came upon a totem, a carved killer whale, and close to the whale a handmade spike. Foliage almost covered it. I started to take it and then thought better of it. I said to Stewie, "I'm afraid to take it without asking Gibert. He's superstitious, you know, and also respectful of the things that belong to the past. Suddenly I feel like a grave robber, and I don't even know it is a grave."

We rowed to the boat. I asked Gilbert if it was all right to take the spike.

Gilbert said, "OK."

We paddled back to shore, pushed through the muskeg and found the spike. Stewie carried it to the skiff. We rowed to the Keeper and went on board with the spike.

In the morning we ran into Steamboat Bay and anchored. Mrs. Don Hamilton and her children were staying in one of the cabins.

Stewie went to play with the children.

About an hour later, one of them came running to tell us Stewie had fallen and was unconscious. We ran, picked him up and carried him to the Keeper. On board in his bunk he lay quiet.

Gil started immediately for Craig. The weather had turned, and the sea was rough. I sat by Stewie, holding him in his bunk and putting wet cloths on his forehead.

When we reached Craig he was still unconscious. As soon as Gilbert tied up to the dock and was free to watch Stewie, I went to the home of the public health nurse, who came to the boat immediately. After examining Stewie she called a doctor in Ketchikan who said he'd send a helicopter after the boy if he didn't feel better soon.

Soon after the nurse was there, Stewie started wakening but was disoriented. About 9 that night he suddenly wakened like himself and was hungry.

I asked how he felt. "Does your stomach hurt? What are you hungry for? Do you have a headache? You were unconscious at Steamboat Bay and we've come to Craig. You've been unconscious all this time."

Stewie had never heard me ask so many questions or sound so worried. He said, "First, Grandma, I feel all right. Second, I'd like anything to eat you'd like to fix."

Gilbert interrupted us. "You know, it was taking the spike that caused this trouble. You shouldn't take things from graves and especially one that belonged to a Native doctor."

I answered, "You said it was all right."

"I'm sorry," Gilbert said. "I didn't pay any attention to you when you came on board to ask me about taking a spike. Besides, you let Stewie carry it. If you were going to take it, you should have carried it yourself."

Stewie said, "I don't believe in that old stuff anyway."

I said, "Your Gramps does. When we go by Doctor Skowl's grave he always says, 'Hurry up and get ready now. We're going to go by Doctor Skowl's grave and you've got to throw him an offering.'"

"Who was Doctor Skowl?" asked Stewie.

"He was the next-to-last Native doctor around," Gilbert said. "George Hamilton remembered him. A Native doctor used methods of treating sicknesses they'd used for hundreds of years. They cured the sick by dancing, drumming or singing, driving away the evil spirits that caused the illness. They had tremendous power, really more than the chiefs.

"They always chose an out-of-the-way place on a waterway to be buried.

"The last Native doctor around sank a great big ship off the dock at Gambier Bay. One of the old, old canneries in Alaska was in Gambier Bay. The rumor is that the ship denied the doctor some kind of privilege—maybe wouldn't let him longshore or something. As she was backing away from the dock, she hit a rock and down she went. Lots of the crew drowned. The people all claimed the shaman, the doctor, did it. I think they called him Gambier Bay Jim."

"Remember," Gilbert said, "I've told you before there were natural explanations for events that seemed mysterious. When I was up in Gambier Bay last time with Carolyn on the Donna S., we got to talking about it. I put the fathometer on, and we ran around the bay. Sure enough, a rock came to a peak.

"In those days there weren't fathometers, and the bays weren't charted as they are now. If the captain or mate on the ship was a little angry when he took off and didn't take his time with his sounding lead, how easily he'd hit the rock."

"And by the way, Stewie," he said, "about your trouble—you probably hit your head when you fell and had a slight concussion."

Chapter II. Big Daykoo

I<small>N</small> 1897, my folks got this mining deal into their heads and moved to Big Daykoo to develop my dad's gold mining claims. My uncle, J. Loomis Gould, and his wife joined their son, Hal, in Hetta Inlet, where they had prospects in the copper mining industry. Their daughter, Vesta, had died earlier. Vesta Bay is named for her.

Amanda McFarland, who had operated a children's home at Howkan since 1886, retired to go south. She was Rebecca Reed Gould's sister.

The store was sold and the sawmill sold to Alex Yeltatzie of the Queen Charlotte Islands.

The public school continued with another teacher than Clara Gould McLeod.

I was 6 when the following story happened at Big Daykoo.

Gilbert and His Dad Find a Body

Duncan, Jimmy Scott and Jimmy's wife came in Duncan's sloop from Klinquan to our place in Big Daykoo. It was in the fall of 1910, right after fishing season, and the weather was beginning to be bad. When weather permitted, Duncan was going to sail on about 25 miles over to Cape Chacon and around Cape Chacon to Ketchikan through Nichols Passage. He was going to order lumber from Heckman to build a gasoline boat. That's when Heckman was the big wheel in Ketchikan.

Duncan and Jimmy Scott anchored their sloop in Little Daykoo. They walked around the beach of Big Daykoo and stayed at our house the night, hoping to start out early the next morning.

I remember in the morning my mother giving Duncan coffee

and breakfast. In those days the white people and Natives always talked Chinook back and forth—Chinook, the trade language. I was 6, and I remember Duncan well because he had a white handkerchief over a missing eye and tied in the back. Duncan was of a high family, so he always wore a cover over his disfigurement.

Duncan that morning said, "Well, I'm going to Ketchikan now. If the wind is right when I come back, I'll stop and see you again."

The folks replied, "OK." As it was still dark, Dad walked over the sand and gravel beach of Big Daykoo with them to Little Daykoo with the lantern.

We were 14 miles from Howkan, the closest town, and at that time of year you didn't get up to town very often and you had few visitors. Maybe a month, or maybe two months after Duncan left, the word was that Duncan and Jimmy Scott and his wife had been lost on the east side of Cape Chacon up at Mallard Bay.

Well, the Haida always wanted to find the body of anyone lost at sea. They believed if they didn't bury the body, the land-otter people took the body's spirit. The spirit was lost and had to roam the woods wild. They all came and looked and looked around Mallard Bay and the east coast of Prince of Wales Island. They finally found one body, so ground up from being in the surf everyone said the body was Duncan's to make the family feel good.

The next spring we had a real bad blow. In March it can be bad and then kind of good. It had been bad, and the wind really blew into Big Daykoo. The day after the blow, my dad said he better go over to Little Daykoo to see how his sloop was that he had anchored there.

I wanted to go along, and my dad didn't want to take me. My mother said, "Take him along." My father did.

The water was at the half-tide mark coming in, and as I walked along with Dad near the woods, I saw something down in the surf going up and down. My dad said, "Oh, something's there."

Sometimes, you know, a big skate or some other fish or animal would die and would float in. We'd found both deer and wolf in the logs.

I said, "That's no skate. It looks like somebody."

My dad couldn't see. He was getting older and had glasses, and today they were fogging up. He said, "You wait here." And he walked down the beach. Then he came back and said, "Let's go home."

We went home. When we got there, he said to my mother, "That's just a great drift pile all along the beach and a body, and that's Duncan's body."

My Aunt Molly was with us then. My mother went with my dad, and my aunt stayed with me and my sisters.

My dad and mother dragged the body up the beach as far as they could. His hands were gone and his head was gone.

I remember how the wolves howled. The body smelled so bad. I guess he'd been frozen in the creek because the corpse was well preserved. He was tattooed on the leg. We don't have anything tattooed that way anymore. It's what the Haida called a "copper plate" and the "highest."

My parents got him up on the beach and piled drift logs around him.

The Canadians were building the town of Prince Rupert, diagonally southeast from Cape Muzon. I guess, from what I've heard, the people had rafted in their lumber to build the village. Some of the timber tied together had broken up and drifted out. As a result, there were always good planks on our beach. Dad made a rough box with the material. Mother and Dad put the body in the homemade coffin and covered it.

George Hamilton was there, and Craig Millar and Eddie came down. They took the body to Howkan. That was the spring of 1911.

The Haida always had to pay for a favor or they didn't feel right. My mother wouldn't take any money for such a thing. Well, us kids had never had any Christmas with presents in our lives. Because of the indebtedness the Duncans felt, next holiday there were more Christmas gifts than I'd ever imagined. As long as old Ben Duncan was alive, I was just like a brother to him. That family never forgot our finding the body.

Gilbert Remembers the Boundary Dispute

In the fall when I was 9 years old, my family came back to Cape Muzon from Howkan to dig our potatoes.

Two Canadian surveyors were camped on the south side of Big Daykoo. There had been a boundary dispute between the United States and England for years. Even when Russia claimed the rights to Alaska, the United States, England and Russia were quarreling over the boundary. In the early 1800s, President Polk was elected with the slogan "Fifty-four forty or fight!", referring to the dispute.

The United States and Canada were trying to settle the controversy, and the two men camped there during the late summer of 1913 were surveying.

I'll never forget the way it rained that night, like pouring buckets and buckets of water on the beach. The wind howled in rhythmic swells, and trees cracked and the surf beat against our fence.

In the morning, Howkan Smith walked along the beach to our house from Little Daykoo. He was living at his shack there and working on his assessment. The whole bay, which is 1½ miles long and a mile wide, was just a mass of trees and mud and sticks and brush from slides. You couldn't even row in it.

Howkan Smith came to the kitchen and said to my dad, "It looks as though that Canadian camp is gone."

My dad and Howkan Smith walked as close to the water as they could through the rubble, back toward Little Daykoo so they could look across to the southern bank. They couldn't see any Canadian camp at all. It was gone.

About a week or so later, a Canadian revenue cutter came in. Its crew searched the whole area and didn't find anything. A week or so after that, a boat, the Old Teddy, built by Captain Forss and Axel Osberg, came. Casey Williams, former chief of police in Ketchikan, came with the crew.

For 30 days they all dug along that southern bank. I remember because they boarded with us. As I recall, they never found a thing of those surveyors other than their boat. [Lewis Green in *The*

Boundary Hunters, a book about the boundary dispute, says the searchers salvaged a pocket watch, a pair of overalls, a sack of flour, a few tins of food and a plate.]

The surveyors had been camped in an alder slide area. After a few days of rain, they had gotten scared and moved to the big timber. The slides came down on both sides of their original location. If they hadn't moved, they wouldn't have been touched. There were 13 slides in 1½ miles.

Chapter III. Howkan, 1911-1915

WHEN I WAS 7, we moved to Howkan. The families were leaving for Hydaburg. There were few children at school, and the big old building was scary. On the first floor, some of the rooms were unused, and at the top of the stairs, two empty rooms with a partition between opened into the hall.

A boxed stairwell came down from that dark region to a landing. Then the steps turned. From there on down, they had only a railing. We all knew that above that closed-in stairway the devil, witches and Stawa [phonetic spelling], the ghost, haunted the rooms and belfry. Every night someone was seeing a ghost someplace in one of the dark paths. There must have been graveyards everywhere.

Early one winter morning, my mother, the teacher, told me to go get some wood. I was chopping on it in the hall when all of a sudden something thudded down those steps. I dropped the ax and ran into the schoolroom yelling, "Stawa!" One boy ran over the top of me getting out.

Well, finally W.E. Ross—Howkan Ross, the store owner—and some others went up. They found out what it was. When I was chopping at the bottom of the stairs, a coil of clothesline wire stored at the top started bouncing down to the landing.

That year was kind of hard. I had never gone to school and had never been around children. Those kids spoke Haida when they weren't in school. I knew very little and that not very good, so I was embarrassed to talk it.

I spoke Chinook, the trade language. Because everybody had a different pronunciation, all persons were comfortable with Chinook.

About the same time my mother came back to Howkan to teach, the Reverend John Brown, the lay minister in Klinquan, was transferred to Howkan. According to my friend Helen Brown Sanderson, his daughter, they were there until 1916 when everyone finally went to Hydaburg, Craig or Ketchikan.

The Browns were transferred to Hydaburg. Their nice house in Klinquan, one year old, had been moved to Howkan and then to Hydaburg. The people did that. They moved their houses on rafts as a whole or in dismantled parts. Helen Sanderson said the missionary houses were fine, with chandeliers.

Helen and I were in "chalk class" together. That's the same as kindergarten or first grade. We wrote on little slates.

Dewey Skulka was my pal, and I guess we were into mischief.

ᐱ ᐱ ᐱ

Matthew Charles of Howkan let me use one of his Native traps to trap mink. The first time I ever caught one, I rowed across Kaigani Strait from Howkan to an island in Bolles Inlet to set the deadfall trap the way Matthew Charles taught me. Sure enough, when I checked it in a few days, it had a mink.

The principle of the deadfall trap is that a pole triggered across the mink trail will fall on the mink and break its back. Because lots of people were careless about going away leaving a trap set, the deadfall trap was outlawed. The steel trap had advantages. It caught more mink. It's easier hidden, but it rusts and won't spring if it's left too long.

But it was the white man's teaching the Natives to pit light at night that decimated the mink and land otter. Using a light and making a sound, a little squeal just like a mink, they called the mink right up to them. When the tide was low and the mink came out to feed, you could call 20 of them up to you. Some men used this for deer, too.

The Villagers of Howkan Often Told the Story About How Luke Frank and Alfred Quiance Skillie Escaped Becoming Land-Otter Men

Fur seal hunting, Luke Frank and Alfred Quiance Skillie [phonetic spelling] had an adventure on the west coast of Dall Island.

With their gear, they canoed down Kaigani Strait, through the vicious tides around Cape Muzon and up the west coast past Port Bazan harbor. They were in the Pacific Ocean.

They knew that treacherous shoreline, but even so they wrecked their boat on one of the rocks, which in Oregon would have been called a sea stack. They scrambled up and lived a couple of days on raw seaweed, kelp and the little blue oval mussels found attached to the rocks. No one could exist long on that diet. They'd not survive just waiting to be rescued. Visions of the land-otter man who would possess them if they died in the water wilderness frightened them. They'd be sentenced to roaming the rest of their lives, half human and half land otter.

So, swimming ashore at low tide, using their rubber boots for life preservers, they finally struggled up on land. Once on the small bit of beach, they rested briefly. Then going north before the tide came in, they hugged the side of the mountain that dropped abruptly into the ocean. Suddenly they saw ahead a creek streaming down from the east, cutting a path for them across the island. From then on, not only did they have a place to walk but food and water were no problem.

At last they straggled onto the beach at Ham Cove. A forsaken weatherbeaten skiff lay there. They were weak and cold, but they took the boat and paddled across Kaigani Strait to Howkan, bailing all the way. At home, they beached the wreck and collapsed.

Their friends came to help. There was great joy that the men weren't lost to forever roam the woods as land otters.

45

Captain Jim Edenso

At Point Bazan, Captain Jim Edenso, a Haida of Howkan, found the body of a man on the beach. It was while the Edensos were out on the coast hunting sea otter on its way to the breeding grounds.

Captain Jim buried the body and marked the place well. He passed the word to the people at the trading post at American Bay, who relayed it to the officials at Sitka.

The Edensos were held in great respect, and the captain was an excellent pilot. Everyone knew it. He was in demand.

Because he found the body and buried it, the American government gave him a commendation and then also gave him a Master's Certificate for first-class pilot. The praise was added, "Captain Jim, you are a civilized Indian!" This was an insult to the Haida people in a way, but they took it with humor and teased Captain Jim about being a "civilized Indian."

Captain Jim was a fine man. By the time I knew him, he was a little dried-up fellow. He used to take the ships north into Klawock and south to Victoria, British Columbia. In fact, he was what nowadays we call a pilot for the Inside Passage. Some of the boats he served on were the Challenge, the Klawock and the Alice, which were cannery tenders, and Craig Millar's Cordova and Klinkwan.

Andrew Natkong

When I was a boy, there was a fellow in Howkan by the name of Andrew Natkong. He had some education. He might have gone to school to my mother a little bit. He built his own boats. He sawed his own lumber. He would go into Ham Cove across from Howkan and he'd fell those bull pine trees, roll them into the creek, tow them down and then tow them across Kaigani Strait to Howkan. Yes, he built his own boats; installed the gasoline engine and even made his own rudder and shoe himself. He did all his own blacksmithing, bored his own holes in the iron by hand. He was a very hardworking, stubborn and intelligent man.

When President Roosevelt called in all the gold, Albert Brown as interpreter went into the bank with Andrew. Harry Sprague was the banker. Andrew had three or four thousand dollars in gold. When they got through, Harry Sprague said to Al, "You don't have to tell that man anything about percentage or banking laws. I don't think you have to do much explaining to him."

Andrew was a great friend of mine, but he was stubborn.

Luke Frank

Howkan, where the houses were, had a gentle sandy beach. The villagers paddled in and pulled up right in front of their homes. Large boats like the steamships and U.S. revenue cutter from Fort Wrangell always dropped their hook for short stops near Mission Cove, south of Howkan proper, but for longer stays they crossed the strait to American Bay at Dall Island.

The cutter may have come regularly. The Coast Guard was the enforcement agency. The United States purchased Alaska in 1867, and the only law in existence until 1884 was a Customs Act, which meant foreign goods were subject to duties and the laws of commerce and navigation applied. The part that affected the most people was prohibition of the importation and sale of liquor.

I have one story about the cutter.

One time, just before the crew landed, Luke Frank threw away his home brew made of vegetables. The chickens drank it and got drunk. The hens soon were lying around with their legs in the air. One rooster tried to crow and croaked and croaked. The saying was if a chicken made a low, hoarse noise like that, it would die or some person would die.

Luke Frank's wife panicked and said to Luke, "Go kill that chicken so no one in the village will pass on. Besides, those Coast Guard men are going to know something's wrong."

He rushed out, looked the chickens over and killed them all. He said, "How would I know for sure which one made the squawk? I had to kill them all."

Chapter IV. Forrester Island

THERE WERE TWO bakeries on Forrester Island, my folks' and the Royalties'.

The crew of the cannery tender had quite a time getting my mother's big old stove ashore in one of the large skiffs when we , moved from Howkan. We had two tents, with wooden floors. We used homemade wooden bunks with hemlock brush for a mattress. Some people had canvas folding cots. There were no sleeping bags, just a bedroll of blankets.

All the newcomers on Forrester Island, mostly Norwegians, camped at the south side of the bite at Wood Cove. Oldtimers from all over the world stayed in the middle at Eagle Harbor, where there was a small freshwater stream. The Alaskans or Natives camped on the north. The newcomers and the Alaskans didn't get along as well as the oldtimers and the Alaskans did. They had worked out a mutually profitable relationship.

On Forrester there are no natural anchorages and no beach, just rocks. The mild-cure station people had rolled the boulders away from shore and put in a big hemlock log slip, drilling down into the rock and fastening it with U-bolts. The slip was 10 feet wide and maybe 60 feet long. Planed with 3-by-12's, it accommodated two rows of nested boats.

Maybe a couple of hundred fishermen were vying for position going out and coming in. Once in the water, moving with the ocean swells, the small boats were an impressive sight.

The fishermen rowed north to Cape Horn Rocks, named after Fred Horn's dad, Bill, I suppose because he got in trouble out there. The Alaskans were superstitious about Lowrie Island, a small island near Forrester. You had to fish it just right or you'd be in trouble.

The Norwegians concentrated around Sea Lion Rock, which used to be called Norwegian Rock.

The fish buyer furnished excitement for the day. The hand-trollers' camps had to be a day's round trip or less from the mild-cure stations so the tenders could get the fresh fish to the station rapidly. The packers and buyers came each day. I remember one—Adam Wilson. He ran the Little Todd. He'd strut into camp and throw down his sack of gold—$1,000 worth of $5, $10 and $25 coins. Then, after talking awhile, he would start making change with the bakery or with the fishermen.

Tongass Trading Co.'s floating store, the Penguin, anchored out. It was operated by a man from Petersburg, Alfred Howe. The stockholders were Fremont and Cane.

German money was behind the mild-cure stations, and the market was primarily German. Craig Millar worked with Hyman H. Bergman, who represented Lindenberger Bros. Fish Co. of Hamburg, Germany. Lindenberger Packing Co. expanded. Not only did they mild cure but also canned and had a cold-storage facility for freezing fish.

When Germany declared war on Russia and on France in the summer of 1914, the handtrolling camps were affected. I don't know why, but everything stopped. For about a week, no packers came to the camp. Finally, the handtrollers who waited were returned as far as Craig by Lindenberger's two big fishpackers, the Orient and the Berlin. The people had to get the rest of the way home the best they could.

One man rowed from Forrester Island 30 miles to the southern tip of Dall Island, past Cape Muzon and then on to Cape Chacon, across to Percy Island and into Ketchikan in a 13½-foot Davis. Ben Jacobsen, who used to be a barber in Ketchikan, rowed to Dall Island, through Meares Passage, down Ulloa Channel and over to Sulzer, put his boat on the mail wagon across the portage and then rowed from Cholmondeley Sound to Ketchikan. (Lindenberger had a plant at Roe Point, near Ketchikan, as well as at Craig.)

Λ Λ Λ

On Forrester Island, there were thousands of gulls, murres, ancient murrelets and petrels. Those birds laid eggs just on the edges of the cliffs—mostly on the ocean side. One thing I'll never forget. About midnight, when they were only a few days old, the murrelets tumbled, scurried and scrambled down the cliffs and straight out to sea. The older birds sat out in the water and called to them, and the babies came in waves, beautiful little black and white chicks.

Sometimes the Alaskans climbed the cliffs for eggs, in season. The murres produced the favorite egg. I guess I already mentioned that Walter Ketah of Klawock was the most famous human egger, which is what they called the people who hunted fresh bird eggs. Hunting the eggs and using them didn't hurt the population of birds; it just delayed the hatching time. The birds, I guess, laid more eggs—just like chickens do when their eggs are taken away from them.

Chapter V.
Gilbert Remembers Sulzer

IN THE EARLY 1900s, many copper mines sprang up along Hetta Inlet. Hetta Inlet extends five miles north from Lime Point on Prince of Wales Island, breaking off from Cordova Bay. Sukkwan Strait opens off Hetta Inlet. Hetta continues on 11 miles to Gould Island and to the head of the passage, where the portage used to be to Cholmondeley Sound.

Copper City and the Corbin Mine were on the eastern shore of Hetta. Five miles above Copper City was Copper Harbor, with Coppermount's smelter at the head of the bay and the salmon cannery on the north. The Cuprite Mine and Sulzer were near the head of Hetta Inlet.

Sulzer was a prosperous settlement with a deep harbor and mining office on pilings, ore bunkers and a powerhouse, all built over the tidelands, and a hotel. A cable tramway ran two miles up to the mine itself.

My mother was cook at the hotel from about 1915 to 1918.

Rosestick Johnny hung out at the Cuprite Mine. He had sticks —divining rods—with which he claimed he located gold. He'd walk over the ground with the rods held in his hands. Where there was ore, the sticks pointed to the ground.

I also remember Harry Brice, King Brice's father. He was in charge of taking supplies from the beach up the aerial tramway to the mine and taking the ore down. The Cuprite Mine wasn't one of the successful operations, and he never got paid.

At Coppermount were two saloons and a few girls. Harry Brice

went there to play the piano. He'd play, "Are you from Dixie? Yes, I'm from Dixie, too." He never got paid for that, either, but everyone enjoyed his music.

ᐱ ᐱ ᐱ

At Copper City was a foreman, Bill Dalton, the meanest man who ever breathed. This fellow, they all claimed, when he was foreman of mines in Butte, Montana, never walked the sidewalks at night. He wended his way down the middle of the street.

We all knew the story of Chris Copstead and Bill Dalton. Their friendship began when Chris Copstead, from Scandinavia, not yet able to speak English, was in the bunkhouse with Bill Dalton and Mulligan Pete, who got into an argument. No one could lick Bill Dalton; however, when the argument turned into a fight and Bill had Mulligan Pete down, beating the heck out of him, Chris Copstead couldn't stand watching a big man abuse a smaller man.

He decided to put a stop to it. He grabbed Bill Dalton. Bill went after Chris, who was small, too, only about half the size of Bill. But Chris was strong. He doubled Bill up and shoved him under the bunk.

From then on, Bill Dalton and Chris were the best of friends. I guess it was the first time old Bill Dalton ever got handled.

Bill ended his life violently. Thirty or 40 years ago or more, when Sam Daniels was still chief of police in Ketchikan, in one of those dark one-room cabins that used to be strung along Thomas Basin on Barney Way, Bill put a 10-gauge shotgun in his mouth and pulled the trigger.

ᐱ ᐱ ᐱ

All Southeast Alaska loved Charley Sulzer, who owned the mine at Sulzer. He had a brother who was governor of New York.

B.D. Stewart, father of Judge Tom Stewart of Juneau, was the superintendent of the mine.

Charley ran against Judge James Wickersham for the job of Alaska's delegate to Congress. Wickersham was territorial Alaska's delegate 14 years. At one of the elections, Wickersham was defeated by Sulzer. At Wickersham's insistence there was a recount, and Wickersham was winner. Maybe because of that, some of the oldtimers from Southeast Alaska could never be proud of the ferry called the Wickersham.

During election days, Charley Sulzer sent the 45-foot mine tender, the Lydia, his private yacht, to all the villages and camps to bring everybody including the trappers in to vote. When we lived at Howkan, my parents came on the yacht to Sulzer to vote.

He was quite a man. He was the first mine owner to have an eight-hour work day for his employees.

The Lydia was the school ground for Bert Davey and me. We both learned to run the engine on her.

Sulzer had a beautiful house, or mansion. The windows from that house, once it was no longer in use, were moved to Charlie Demmert's home in Klawock.

Because there was not the need for copper after World War I, the mine was slowing up.

Charley was at Sulzer when he got sick. He was taken to Ketchikan by boat, and he died between Metlakatla and Ketchikan before the boat got to the hospital.

Rastus Brown

Rastus Brown came from Nome, hitching a ride on the Sea Wolf. It was in the morning she came slowly up Hetta Inlet to Sulzer, just barely moving, powered by a gas engine and making three or four knots.

Bert Davey and I were on our way to school. We did go sometimes. We saw the tiny two-masted gas schooner, the foremast 'way shorter than the mainmast, and she had no pilot house. The wheel was on the deck, and she had little freeboard. She was about 55 feet long with a 26-foot beam. We'd never seen anything like her, and we ran to the dock to wait and help tie her up.

As she came to the dock, we saw Rastus for the first time. He was no bigger around than the mast and 'way over six feet tall. I still remember how he looked standing there and how impressed I was.

When she pulled up to the dock, the skipper, Harry Osberg, was at the wheel. The crew threw us one quarter-inch-square walrus-hide line, a heaving line with a leather-covered weight attached to the end. It uncoiled as it fell on the deck from the sailor's left hand. Then they pulled up the head line, a 2½-inch rotten rope, and fastened the stern line. Now that she was tied up, we could see she was pretty dilapidated and needed paint and care.

Harry Osberg said, "What place is this?"

Bert and I said together, "Sulzer."

The skipper said, "Where the hell is Sulzer? Close to Ketchikan?"

I answered, "Three miles up to the head of the portage; three miles across the portage and then so many miles down through Cholmondeley Sound and then 35 miles on into Ketchikan."

"Well," Harry Osberg replied, "I can't go there that way. How about by water?"

Bert and I said, "It's 100 and some miles around Cape Chacon."

Harry sighed. "Didn't I come around Cape Chacon?"

"No," Bert said. "Where did you come from?"

"Oh, I'm 64 days out of Cape Nome. I came by an island and then by a cape and then turned and came on in."

"Well," I said, "you came by a cape that must have been Cape Muzon, and the island must have been Forrester Island you saw." Harry looked at us with his one brown eye and his other eye almost blue and didn't say anything.

It seemed the boat belonged to Wittenburg of Nome. He'd been trading with the Sea Wolf in the Gulf of Anadyr, off Siberia. All in all she'd been 21 years in the Arctic, and all their charts for other waters were a thing of the past. They brought her down to Southeast Alaska for engine work. One of the cylinders was cracked. The crew had taken the piston out, and her 30-horsepower Union engine was running on one cylinder. It was time to lay her up.

Harry decided he couldn't take the boat back down around

Cape Chacon to Ketchikan. He talked to whoever was in charge at Sulzer, maybe Dan Raffleton, and got permission to put the boat on the beach over there at Old Man Shellhouse's and leave it there for the winter. As you see, Old Man Shellhouse had one of the few beaches where Osberg could leave the Sea Wolf safely.

The crew unloaded the barrels of skins and stuff, whatever they'd been trading for with the Eskimos in Siberia. They had salted hides and coho salmon and other things. They shipped the cargo out on the mailboat from Wrangell with Walter Walters, who had the mail contract then.

Then they waited for a big tide and beached the Sea Wolf.

They stayed at the hotel and ate there, where Mother was the cook. They were Harry Osberg, two stateside crew members, one Eskimo crew and Rastus, who'd bummed the ride. After they got the boat beached, the captain and two crew members took off across the portage with the man who had the portage mail contract. They left the Eskimo to watch the boat, and they ditched Rastus.

Now Rastus was stranded, and he got a job helping Charley Nelson's dad, Harry Nelson, who was the bull cook at the hotel and who did other jobs like taking care of the furnace and raising the pigs to feed the miners. Rastus was around Ketchikan 50 years after that, and he was always a good guy and a good friend of mine. He never earned a living, working. Probably the only time he ever worked in his life was the winter in Sulzer.

In the spring, Harry Osberg, the crew and the son of Wittenberg all came back. The hotel was shut down, and Mother boarded the men at our house till they got the Sea Wolf in the water and took her to Juneau for a new engine. Because of the Russian Revolution they couldn't trade in Siberia any more, and when the Sea Wolf went back to Nome she took the mail run between Kotzebue and Nome. The last I was in Nome, parts of her were lying in the Snake River there.

As long as there was work, Rastus stayed around Sulzer, but the mine didn't run full-scale after that winter. Now that World War I was over, there was no use for the copper.

I remember one adventure I had with Rastus at Sulzer before he went to Ketchikan.

The year I'm telling about, in good weather the mail carrier drove a team—Chip and Babe and wagon—over the 3½ miles from Cholmondeley Sound to the beginning of Portage Bay. However, in the winter when the snows came, the carrier walked the route with the mail tied to his horse, like a pack horse, or the carrier walked with the mail on his own back. He had to make the trip twice a week, once with local mail for the mines and once to make connections with the Glenora going north to Wrangell.

When the mailman, Jacob Lauth, didn't show up on time in Sulzer, where his family lived, his wife worried. This time she came to my mother's house to ask her to do something. The two of them went to B.D. Stewart, the superintendent, and Stewart sent Rastus, Bert Davey and me to look for the mail carrier.

We took the Lydia up Sulzer Passage and Portage Bay until we came to ice and could go no farther. Just as we were about ready to go back, along the bank came the mail carrier struggling through the snow with one sack of mail. The other two he'd left tied to the horse up the beach. The horse was just too tired to go on.

Rastus and I took the skiff ashore and walked to the horse, and Bert Davey edged the boat along following as far as he could. We found the animal eating kelp on the beach. Rastus, being from Texas, loved and understood horses, and this one was in such bad shape Rastus was sad. The boat people of Alaska, and this mail carrier, really didn't understand about horses and thought they'd survive like deer. This one really showed it. If Rastus had had a gun, he would have shot it to put it out of its misery right then.

The man told us he'd left a worn-out Japanese fellow in the barn at the head of the portage. The fellow wanted to connect with the mail boat going north to Waterfall, where he had a job cooking at the mild-cure station. He had barely made it over the trail, collapsing at the barn while the mail carrier muddled on.

After we'd rescued all the sacks of mail, Bert, Rastus and I ran the carrier on the Lydia to Sulzer. After we deposited him, we went back into Portage Bay as far as we could, anchored the boat, rowed the dinghy ashore and walked the trail along the bank through five or six feet of snow.

We started in the dark, and it seemed even darker and colder by the time we got to the barn. The man, shivering with fear and frost, sat in the old lean-to of a barn with no light or fire. He was glad to see us. The weight of the snow had cracked some of the rafters of the building, and we got an open fire going on the gravel floor, first by whittling off some of the old rafter, dry as powder. We did have flashlights, but because we had to save batteries we didn't use them much. Batteries didn't last the way they do now.

The fire warmed the man. We made tea from melted snow water and heated the sausage bologna he had. After he ate, we started down, half carrying him. Rastus gave him heck all the time. "Take a rest. Take a rest. We'll get you there," Rastus would say. Rastus was tall and strong, making about two of the little fellow. When we finally got down to Sulzer, it was near daylight. The poor man was so overjoyed he gave us each $10.

He said, "If I had lots of money I'd give it all to you."

We all said, "Oh, that's all right." We were happy enough with the $10.

Rastus in Ketchikan

In Prohibition days, Rastus with his sailboat the Pendelope would go down to Prince Rupert to get whiskey to bring to Ketchikan for sale. This night he was coming up and there wasn't much wind for his mast. He was puffing along with the engine. He was through Dixon Entrance and was entering Revillagigedo Channel. There was little sea and swell, so he thought he had it made. He was wrong. The U.S. Coast Guard was out there spotting for him. Rastus identified the Coast Guard boat and went up into Very Inlet going east through Foggy Bay. Foggy Bay is on the mainland south of Behm Canal and across from Duke Island. You can go into the inlet about three miles in a northeast direction by small boat. The narrow inlet widens into a basin, good anchorage for Rastus' small boat.

The crew of the Coast Guard vessel apparently said to themselves, "We'll drop anchor at this main entrance into Very Inlet. Rastus can't get out in the morning without going by us." They had gone in far enough to see Rastus' light in the basin. In the morning, the crew couldn't see his boat. "Well," the watchman said, "I saw the light. Just before daylight that light was still there."

They launched a lifeboat, and into the inlet and basin they rode. There was no Pendelope there. There was a lantern. Rastus had hung a lantern over the limb of a tree on one of the islets and then had snuck out past them in the night. They caught her at Mary Island under sail and with the engine running, too. They came alongside and looked the vessel over. No whiskey. Rastus had already ditched it.

Rastus told me about the Coast Guard commander, who was the finest man Rastus had ever known. The Coast Guard commanders at the Ketchikan Coast Guard base were the ones who chased the rum-runners. This one had Rastus' boat searched more than once. He was a law enforcer who would have pinched his own brother if the brother had done something illegal. What Rastus admired about the man was once he searched your boat and you came through clean, that was it. He never sent anybody later to try to trick you into selling some booze. In other words, he never used entrapment.

He had never spoken directly to Rastus. When the Coast Guard crew came on board the Pendelope, the commander stayed on the bridge of his own boat. The crew had never found any of Rastus' liquor.

Rastus not only smuggled from Canada but also bought from other bootleggers in town.

It was common practice for fishermen to go to Prince Rupert to sell their halibut. Better prices were available there. Many of those men came back with liquor. All the rum-runners carried the bottles in gunnysacks with rocks, so they could dispose of them in a hurry if they were pursued. They'd be sure, with the rocks in the bottom of the sack, that it would all sink.

One high-liner fisherman in Ketchikan, whenever he went into a restaurant, took as many paper napkins as he'd dare. Someone let the cat out of the bag as to what this man did with the napkins. He'd coil up the line fastened to the sack of booze. On the end of the line he had a cork float like seine boats use. He'd take this coil and tie it to the cork float with napkins. In three or four days the napkins fell apart, the cork came to the surface, and he'd pull up the sack. Because Bar Harbor was pretty shallow, he sunk his booze there most often.

Back to the Coast Guard commander. One night Rastus was walking along the street on his way to his boat at Thomas Basin. The commander drove his car up alongside Rastus and slowed up to stop. Some people came out on the street. He cruised on by and around the block past Tongass Trading Co. and Heckman's. Then he was back alongside Rastus near Ohashi's and Thomas Basin. The fellow opened his car window.

"Brown?" he said. "Do you know where a man could get a bottle of good whiskey?"

Rastus looked the other way and said, "Yes. If you go up to Barney Way to such and such a house in half an hour, there will be a sack with it on the porch."

The car drove away.

Rastus went to the bootlegger in Barney Way. Old-time Barney Way is gone now. There used to be two rows of one- and two-room cabins along the south bank of Thomas Basin.

Rastus told this bootlegger, "I want a bottle of Scotch and a bottle of rum and half a dozen of those quart bottles of Canadian beer. Put it in a gunnysack and put it on the porch for a customer."

The bootlegger objected.

Rastus said, "Do it."

The bootlegger agreed but said, "You sit right here till the buyer comes."

In just 30 minutes from the time Rastus had seen the officer on the street, a car drove up. Rastus and the bootlegger heard the footsteps along the boardwalk to the porch; then they heard a clink and footsteps back to the car. The car drove away. They went out to look. The sack was gone, and the money was there.

Rastus said, "I always admired the guy. If he'd ever caught me with whiskey on the boat, I wouldn't have felt bad. He never snuck around. Not him. He was honorable in the way he searched."

⋀ ⋀ ⋀

Rastus and a guy we'll call Jake were in the back room of the Pioneer Cafe, where many had planned their rackets. Rastus was making a deal with Jake, who had worked for the rum-runner they were plotting to hijack. Rastus knew he was dealing with a crook of the worst sort, one who would double-cross anyone. He said to Jake, "You know, I just don't trust you exactly."

All the time Jake was talking, Rastus had his hands under the table. "And," continued Rastus, "don't be pulling any funny stunts on me like you're doing to this guy we're conniving against and you're double-crossing. It won't do you any good."

Jake looked under the table and saw Rastus had a .44 aimed right in the middle of Jake's stomach.

⋀ ⋀ ⋀

In the 1930s, when the booze business slowed down because of the end of Prohibition in 1933, Rastus went into fish pirating. It was new. Big-shot cannerymen were stealing from each other, but the common man wasn't yet robbing traps. Birch Bay Adams, a fellow from Washington, Sharkey Valclem and Rastus were among the first.

Because it wasn't fast enough and had no hatch for fish and ice, the sloop the Pendelope wasn't good for fish pirating. Rastus got a new boat called the Islander, built by the Clarey brothers of Strait Island. The Clarey brothers had a fox ranch on Strait Island in Sumner Strait. They were the only ones, I guess, who ever made money at fox ranching.

The Clarey brothers built the Islander from a knocked-down kit they'd ordered from the Lower 48. The windows were plate glass from the Mariposa, wrecked on Vanderbilt Reef northwestward of Sentinel Island Light. The engine was a Stern, a yacht-type fast engine.

Rastus used his boat a lot, going through two engines. At last he sold his boat and hung around Ketchikan doing nothing. He was not a drinker or a wino—just a non-worker. Except for that winter in Sulzer, he probably never did an honest day's work in his life. If he'd had to work for a dollar, it would have been worth only a dime to him. He just didn't believe in legitimate work.

Chapter VI. Fishermen

Handtrollers supplied the first salteries and mild-cure stations. Trollers with power gurdies started after the handtrollers.

Then there were the purse seiners and the gillnetters and finally the traps. They caught the same kind of fish: red salmon or sockeye, pinks or humpbacks, and silvers or cohos.

There were advantages to trap-caught salmon. Theoretically, there could be control over how many were caught. The quality was better. The fish were prime and could stay in salt water in their habitat until the tenders picked them up to take them directly to the cannery for processing.

The gillnetters and seiners felt the traps had an unfair advantage. Regulations kept the fishermen away from the mouths of rivers and streams. Traps were placed at the good spots to intercept schools of fish. When the traps produced plenty of fish, the canneries wouldn't buy seine fish.

In 1895, James Robert Heckman, then superintendent of the Alaska Packers Association Cannery at Loring, supervised construction of the first commercial fish trap in southeastern Alaska. In 1910, he built and placed in operation the first floating trap. They came in common use about 1917, maybe a bit earlier. After statehood for Alaska in 1959, most of the traps were eliminated.

Handtrollers

My definition for a handtroller I think is the only definition. The fisherman who worked his line by hand with no mechanical help was a handtroller.

He put his cotton line, or cuttyhunk, with a sinker, leader and fresh herring in the water from a spool in the bottom of the boat.

He fastened to the railing a small cedar limb, like a Y, called the watchman, which stuck up six or eight inches above. After he had the amount of line he desired, he'd tie a loop and put it over the watchman. This way his hands were free to row. When the stick wobbled, a fish was on. Sometimes the fisherman would give the line a pull with his hands, after a stroke with his oars, to give the bait more action.

They used salted herring sometimes, but fresh herring was plentiful. The oldtimers always carried a herring rake in their rowboats. The herring rake was split-off cedar. The fisherman drilled holes in his piece of cedar and put in brass wires and filed them into sharp points. He'd stand paddling in the front of the boat, holding the herring rake with the sharp points in. In a school or ball of herring, he'd turn the sharp ends toward the herring, pierce them and bring the rake up to the boat with them, squirming, impaled on the tines.

Near a kelp bed, he'd put the bulb from the brown kelp in his boat, fastening it there. The offshore kelp bed was important in places like Forrester Island. The holdfast or stipes of seaweed quieted the ocean waters and protected the little boat.

The Haida canoe was a good handtrolling boat. Rod Davis and his father, from Metlakatla, built hundreds of round-bottomed boats for the handtrolling fleet. The 16-foot Davis carried the fisherman's little camp stove, his tent, blankets, grub, rifle and frow to split out cedar. Some men put sails on their skiffs and went from fishing camp to fishing camp in their seaworthy Davises. Others were towed or hitched a ride with the cannery tenders. As late as 1954, Pete Holmberg of Ketchikan built wooden round-bottomed outboards resembling the Davis.

The early skiffs had a special seat called the dry seat. The men hewed out a piece of wood that had a crook, laced the open place with rawhide or good twine and fit it to the boat. When rain or ocean swells came over the side, the men sat dry. The water dripped down through the lacing. In addition, the seat was springy, more comfortable than a plank.

Adventure on Brokey Joe's Island

Isaac Rose, a packer from Waterfall Cannery to Forrester Island, on one of his trips made a side visit to Craig, the "Little Chicago" of the west coast. Leaving from there, he and Joe McGrath and Annie Foss from Prince Rupert, who was going out to visit her husband, fishing on the Todd with Adam Wilson, all were drunk. The Rose blew up, and Annie Foss was sitting on the hatch and she sailed overboard. Joe McGrath jumped in, got hold of her and swam back to the boat. Isaac by then had the skiff in the water, and they all got in the dinghy and rowed ashore to Brokey Joe's Island. As time would tell, Isaac must have had the company's $1,700 in gold pieces, the fish-buying money, but when they were picked up hours later, there was no money.

Well, Isaac came back to Craig the next year, and he borrowed old Sig's boat. He'd say he was going to get fish to eat, and he'd be gone a couple of days. He'd come back, down at the mouth. And he'd go again. Craig people thought Isaac, before his rescue, had hidden Wiesa Packing Co.'s gold and because he was drunk at the time and burned pretty bad couldn't remember where he'd hid it, so he kept trying to find the sack of coins.

A year later, the Skulkas were on their way to Fish Egg Island, a tiny island right at Craig, in Trocadera Bay. Before Craig existed we called the area "Fish Egg." The Haida and Tlingit always went there after the first long runouts after Saint Patrick's Day. No matter what the Fish and Wildlife say, after Saint Patrick's Day, when the tide has those long runouts, the herring start to spawn.

In the middle of the herring spawn, we always have dirty weather. The Haida knew an afternoon west or northwest squally wind and hard thunderstorms chased the Thunderbird out to the ocean. Then we're supposed to have good weather. So, the Haida people, after going through the Skookum Chuck and through Ulloa Channel, often stopped to camp at Brokey Joe's sandy beach for the night and then crossed to Craig or Fish Egg Island in the morning when the water was still. Thomas Skulka, his son-in-law

Peter Johns, and two of Thomas' children, Violet and Dewey, did just that, pulled their canoe up on the good beach at Brokey Joe's.

As soon as the Skulka family beached the canoe, Dewey looked for a spruce tree with pitch to build a fire. The first thing the Haida did when they camped was to chop into a spruce tree so the sap would come out. No matter how rainy or stormy, whenever you found a tree that had the resin, you could chop in and get the dry wood inside to start the fire. They chose a tree with a little lean to it. That tree would have pitch because it was crying at leaning.

Also, there was one special substance out of some spruce trees the kids always chewed like gum. I've tried it lots of times. It's the redbud pitch, kind of hard to chew and not at all soggy.

Anyway, Dewey was getting the pitch, and he saw a corner of a sack Raven had been pulling on. Raven smells anything human beings have had. Dewey pulled the canvas sack out, and there were many $20 gold pieces. He took a handful down to the canoe to show Peter Johns. Dewey said, "Is this money?" They all went to look. The sack was pretty well rotted, and 80 more $20 gold pieces lay on the ground, 85 in all.

The next few days, the family half-heartedly collected fish eggs and then hurried home. They discussed among themselves what they should do about the gold. They heard the insurance company had paid off Wiesa Packing's loss of Isaac Rose's fish-buying coins.

Dewey told me about it, and his father, who told my mother everything, talked it over with her. They decided the fair thing would be to give the money to the cannery, who in turn gave them the boat the Verbas Unitas, and no one said a word during the whole transaction.

Thaddeus and I Rob a Creek

One year the fish were scarce, and the seiners, who couldn't by law get near the mouths of the creeks where the fish schooled, felt it wasn't fair. The traps, located at strategic spots, filled up. Between Craig and Klawock in the bay were one pile trap and three floaters in six miles on one side, and on the other were two floating traps. Nakat Packing at Waterfall had 21 traps, one every mile where the fish were traveling.

I remember one time. I'd had the Delaware a year or two. It was Sunday, and no fishing was allowed. We'd come down by 'Frisco Point between Noyes and Lulu islands. There were fish all over the flats at the mouth of the creek.

The Daycanoe dropped anchor near us, and the skipper, Thaddeus Isaacs, rowed over to us. He said, "Gilbert, are you going to try to make a set now?"

I said, "Come aboard, Thaddeus." He did. "Why don't we make a set?" I said. "I'll take half of your crew with mine. We can work fast. I'll make a set with the skiff. As soon as we get the rings up, you come with the Daycanoe, which is shallower than the Delaware. You tow us out, and then we'll brail the fish and divide them."

"Well," he said, "I'll have to go ask Tecumseh." Tecumseh was the cannery owner's—Bob Peratrovich's—representative, and he was on the Daycanoe.

Thaddeus and I went over to have a talk in Chinook with Tecumseh. We decided to fish together.

We made a set and were towed out and were brailing. Tecumseh and I each had 2,500 fish. Tecumseh patted me on the back and said what a great thing we had done.

I said, "You're a loyal Salvation Army member. How about it? How come you think it's OK we broke the law?"

"Yes," he said, "in the eyes of man, that's the way it is. In the eyes of the Lord, it isn't. If the Lord didn't want us to have the fish, the Diamond C. would have been here before us." The Diamond C. was just coming in with a jealous skipper. "It's all right, or we wouldn't have the fish. That law is man's. It wasn't made by nature. You sleep tonight, and don't figure that you have broken the law at all." He laughed.

∧ ∧ ∧

I Was a Fish Pirate

One time I eased my boat alongside the trap of a watchman I knew well. I propositioned him to buy some fish.

"No," he said, "I've been selling all I dare, and besides, there's a tender coming tonight and I've got to have some for the company. Go someplace else to get your fish."

We crossed to another trap through the sloppy sea. We threw a line over the cleat and took the boat out of gear. She took a beating lashed to the trap. Three of the crew leaped to the trap and started dickering with the watchman. They called to me, "Don't worry. He's agreed to take the money. Start to brail." [Gilbert didn't tell me this, but they were probably shining the gillnetter's spotlight in the trapman's eyes. MLS] The crew took the cable from the winch and attached it to the spiller.

Traps are basically boxes of chicken wire with rocks on the bottom to hold them down. They are hooked to logs that lie floating at the top over other logs. The last rectangle the fish go in is called a spiller, which might be 25 feet square with ropes on the top. There are two ways to take the fish from the spiller. One is with a hoop, and the other is with the power brailer on the boat. We were using the boat brailer.

I started the winch. We had loaded the boat about two-thirds full, right on the deck, when we saw a vessel in the distance.

I yelled a warning: "Let's get out of here!" We cleared our lines. I turned off the winch and called to the mate. He threw the boat in gear and went full speed ahead.

Then I realized that Jumbo, who had pulled the brailer, was still on the trap. He had thrown the line off the cleat, but he hadn't gotten aboard. We swung around and ran full speed, so close I don't know to this day why our propeller didn't hit the cable that goes off the head anchor of the trap. Jumbo, as agile as a sea lion, jumped, grabbed our rig and came aboard.

It was such a narrow escape I knew I'd think twice before trying that again.

70

Hank Adams and the It

There was one old fellow, Hank Adams, who had a boat called the It. The boat was still afloat in the '60s, but Hank was dead.

In the early days, he had run Chinese men across the border at Blaine, Washington. Hank looked like Santa Claus, not the real tough guy he was.

He was an old man when he came to Noyes Island. Every morning he'd be in with the It loaded with fish. Big Andy Gunderson, the superintendent, who had known Hank for years, would come down to the dock and say, "Got fish, Hank?"

"Oh, I got a few, Andrew. I got a few," Hank would say softly.

"Did you get them out of my traps?"

"Huh? Fish out of your traps? Oh, no, Andrew. I wouldn't do anything like that, because I'm bringing them to sell to you."

We all knew that's exactly where he got them.

⚠ ⚠ ⚠

The tender and/or barge or scow brailed the fish from the trap. As the scow made its way to the cannery, the gillnetters would run alongside. One man would go on the scow and scoop fish over to the fishing boat. Once it was loaded, the captain would run ahead of the tender to sell the fish to the very cannery that owned the tender.

Sometimes pirates sold to another cannery than the one owning the trap. Many of the cannery owners knew their boats were fish-pirating. That was great sport for them—to can somebody else's fish.

Trouble Near the Mouth of a Creek

This seiner I knew had a boat about half-loaded with salmon too near the mouth of the creek. The fisherman saw the Fish and Wildlife boat coming in. He knew the crew could tell from a long way off he was inside the markers. He told his men to go on to bed. He went below to the engines and let a lot of gasoline run out of the carburetor. When the Fish and Wildlife men got close to the seiner, now smelling of gasoline, the seiner captain was waving at them to come on in. They were coming, all right, and they arrested him. The fish warden told him to start the engine to go to Craig.

"No," he said, "I'm broke down. That's why I was gesturing you to come in. I can't run my engine."

The warden said, "OK, we'll tow you, all right. Don't worry about that."

So the enforcement vessel took the seiner in tow to Craig. They went first to Libby's Cannery and pitched off the fish.

The fishing crew was to report to the court at 10 o'clock the next morning. The seiner captain appeared at court on time. He had a piece of canvas over a deck bucket he carried.

When he was called before the judge, he said, "Judge. This is Exhibit A."

Well, the judge looked at him with a soul-searching look.

The Fish and Wildlife employee got up before the court and told how he'd found this boat a mile or so inside the closed area. The captain had fish aboard, he said, and water was running out of the seine.

"Yes," the captain said, "that's right. But I had to run in there. That was the closest place to anchor when my engine went haywire. I fixed it the best way I could and ran in there for protection. When I saw the Fish and Wildlife coming, I signaled for help.

"I know water was running out of the seine. You know, Judge, those seines burn in the sun; so I had to pour water on it."

"Can I have one witness?" he asked.

The judge said, "Yes."

"I want the chief engineer off the Fish and Wildlife boat," the seiner said.

The judge answered, "OK," and called the engineer to the stand.

The seiner captain opened the bucket he had carried in. He had a carburetor and the metal float. According to his story, the metal float had sprung a leak, and he had whittled a cork float. He put that in. He said to the chief engineer, "Chief, how long do you think that little Chrysler engine would have run with that cork float?"

"Well, till that cork got so heavy with gasoline that it sank. Then your engine would have flooded."

The captain said, "Thank you. That's what I did. When the original float broke, I put this cork float on and ran to the closest place to anchor safely. That's why we were anchored there, Judge."

The judge turned the fishing boat skipper loose. The Fish and Wildlife warden was mad. He jumped the engineer, who told him, "I only went by what I'd seen. I was under oath. The skipper put it over on you. He certainly did."

"Hero" Bill

This was about 1924. I'll call the fellows Bill and his brother Joe. Joe was outside boss for a cannery. To impress Joe, Bill planned to expose the fish pirates who were among the gillnetters and seiners who sold to Joe. To accomplish this, he became friendly with all the fishermen. He'd say, "When I'm placed on a trap as watchman, come around and see me." He was implying he'd sell them fish from the trap.

Bill became a trapman that summer. Some of the pirates took him up on his offer. They came around in the evening to the trap for fish. He said, "No. No. There isn't enough. You guys go away."

The crew on one boat answered, "You said to come when there were fish. Now you've got fish, and we're going to take them."

Bill got tough. He ran into the trap house, got his rifle and was ready to shoot the gillnetter's spotlight. The captain of the boat said to the first mate, "Let's go. I don't want to get into any shooting business."

While they were backing away, Bill decided he wanted to make a big hero of himself. He fired a shot up in the air. He thought, "A better story for my brother."

The skipper running the gillnetter was a nice fellow, but when he didn't like something he had a bad temper. After he had eased the boat away, he ran to his pilot house and came back with his 30/06 and aimed it at Bill. Bill ran into the trap house. The skipper emptied his gun into the shack. None of the bullets hit Bill. However, one bullet hit the corner of the old-fashioned cast-iron stove, and a chunk of iron from it cut Bill in the hind end. It was painful.

Soon after daylight a seine boat came by. Bill was outside, waving a towel for the boat's crew to stop. They took him to the cannery.

The superintendent called the Coast Guard by wireless. They took Bill to the hospital, where he had stitches. They hunted down the boat and arrested the crew for fish pirating and the skipper for shooting.

A few years later, Bill's brother Joe was promoted from outside boss to superintendent. Bill was still working for the brother, and whenever Joe went away, Bill unofficially took over.

A bunch of Tlingit men and Haida men were hanging their seines at the cannery. Hanging their seines meant they were attaching a float line of corks to the netting, to hold the end of the net on the surface of the water, then attaching the lead weights or lead line to the webbing so part of the net would sink. In the old days, the cannery owned all the gear and paid the fishermen to assemble it.

Bill said to one of the men, "How long is it going to take you to finish hanging that seine?"

"Oh, I don't know," the fisherman said.

"Well, it don't look like you've done much since I was here."

The fisherman said, "Maybe not too much."

Bill went away. Soon he came back and started in again.

The fisherman said, "If you're the boss now, call me a plane."

Bill said, "What do you want a plane for?"

"I want to go get this guy who shot you to come down and shoot you in the hind end again, so you'll leave me alone."

That did it. Bill took off and never bothered them again.

Management's Greed

When Art Wadhams from Nakat Packing retired and lived in Ketchikan, he always sat on the third stool from the door at the Foc's'le Bar.

This fall I went in. "Buy you a drink, Mr. Wadhams?"

"OK," he said. "Well, Gil," he said, "how did you make it this summer?"

"I think the worst I have ever done," I said. "Between us creek robbers and your traps, we got all the fish."

Mr. Wadhams answered, "No. It was never the fishermen or the traps that killed off the fish. It was our management, our greedy people. When you worked for me at Rose Inlet in 1916, you knew the 10th of August was the peak of the runs, wasn't it?"

"It was considered so."

"Even though there were lots of fish coming in and going up the creeks," Mr. Wadhams said, "the boats lay at the dock and the traps were closed, once the cannery had all the fish it could handle.

"Now when the big run is in and there are more fish than one cannery can process, the management calls another cannery: 'We got more fish than we can use,' and the tenders and scows are loaded with the extra and sent to the canneries in another area, canneries not getting fish right then. So all are running full blast.

"You can regulate the fishermen and the traps, but you can't regulate the canneryman's greed."

Carolyn Meets Gilbert
(Carolyn's Story)

My dad had a halibut schooner named the Majestic. In the wintertime, off-season for halibut, he'd pack herring. That means he'd take herring from the boats on the fishing grounds back to the cold storage plants in Ketchikan. He worked for Big Andy Gunderson, who had the contract with both New England Cold

Storage and "Uptown" Cold Storage or Ketchikan Cold Storage, which had a plant right on the downtown waterfront where Tongass' newest building is.

This January, in the 1920s, Dad was going from Ketchikan to Klawock.

(Gilbert interrupted, "In the wintertime, schools of herring come to the inside waters from the ocean and stay near their spawning grounds. In January or February is the best fishing for them, before their eggs and roe develop.")

Because the weather was so bad that time of year, my dad didn't want me to go along. He had to go down around Cape Chacon into Dixon Entrance and up into Cordova Bay.

Until we got away from Ketchikan, I hid out in the fo'c'sle under the galley table. When I finally went up on deck and my dad saw me, he was provoked. Anyway, he went on to Klawock.

In Klawock Bay there was trouble. Because two boats were fishing herring with nets, the local people were getting mad. On our packer, we did have a big seine, but we weren't going to use it. We were just buying herring to be frozen for bait.

Forty or 50 men came out to our boat and made us leave. We went to Craig, on the south end of Klawock Inlet. It was icy out. Dad didn't want to leave me on the boat. He took me to the pool hall while he went to call the governor to get permission to start packing herring. In those days in territorial Alaska, the governor was accessible to everyone.

While I was sitting in the pool hall, all the lights went out. The town generator turned off at 10 o'clock. Tonight, for some reason, the auxiliary light, the gasoline tank with the mantle, wasn't filled. The men just kept on playing cards with a flashlight. I had never seen so many tough-looking men in my life. I sat by the door, petrified, ready to run.

The governor gave us permission to pack herring. The next day we went back to the inlet and bay. The boat Gilbert was fishing on came over and unloaded, pouring the herring on the deck. That's the first time I met him.

Before Dad ever got back to Ketchikan, I had a thrill. Going back we ran into heavy seas and had to dump all the fish on deck overboard.

I should have been scared, but I never was, on the boat with Dad or with Gilbert. I love it all.

They Always Returned Favors

This is a story about a fine old Tlingit who always minded his own business but who had to return favors. After all, that's what the potlatch was all about—a form of insurance, gifts to everyone, who would then have to compensate at some future time.

Once when I was 19 and running the Delaware before she was mine, going through Meares Passage at the north of Dall Island to Forrester Island to pick up fish for Noyes Island Cannery, I turned back because of the fog. A drifting boat came into view, blowing its whistle to avoid an accident in the mist. The Delaware came alongside the powerless boat, Pete's Banshee, high boat in Warm Chuck Cannery. Pete had broken the rudder, which had fallen against the propeller so he couldn't steer. But he could run the engine with the clutch out and pump air for the whistle.

Pete asked if we were going into Craig or Klawock.

I answered that we had set out for Forrester Island but had to turn around to go back to Noyes Island Cannery. We could go to Craig, which we did with the Banshee in tow.

Long after, whenever I was on the fishing grounds, if Pete had fresh meat, he always came alongside and talked to me.

"Got any meat?" he'd say.

"No, we didn't kill a deer," I'd answer, or maybe, "We didn't kill a deer, but yesterday . . ." Then Pete would give me something. He never forgot and always was returning the kindness.

Dutch Uncle

The Fourth of July in Craig was a big day. Although there were no liquor stores in Craig even before Prohibition, there was liquor.

I was fishing herring with Big Andy Gunderson on the Pirate, and Dutch Uncle was the cook. We were tied up at Craig. Big Andy and Dutch Uncle were uptown drinking moonshine they'd gotten from Wrangell. Dutch Uncle met up with Dago Joe and got into a squabble. When Dutch Uncle came down to the dock to the Pirate, he was bragging to beat heck. He said, "I fixed that damn Dago Joe once and for all. I really beat him up."

Dutch Uncle lay down on the hatch and went to sleep.

Denver Moss was also fishing on our boat. He took the lid off the stove in the galley. They always burned coal on the boats in those days. Coal makes soot. Denver Moss took the soot off the lid and blacked Dutch Uncle up good with two black eyes. Dutch Uncle was really passed out and didn't waken.

After awhile, Big Andy woke Dutch Uncle. "What's this I hear about you and Dago Joe having a fight?"

"Oh, I cleaned up on him. I fixed him," said Dutch Uncle.

"Well, it looks like you were the one got fixed." Big Andy put the looking glass in front of Dutch Uncle.

When he saw his black eyes, he was savage. He went uptown looking for Dago Joe, but I don't think he found him.

(Carolyn said: "You don't want to tell the whole story, do you?" She continued: "Dutch Uncle put a burning newspaper under the house where Dago Joe was sleeping off his bender. Dutch Uncle tried to smoke out Joe and caused considerable damage. The marshal threw Dutch Uncle into the clink.")

᭙ ᭙ ᭙

I was fishing herring on the Gladys, and we were coming into the cove in Craig to tie up. Everybody, maybe half the town, with more people coming, was on the dock. I said, "What's all the excitement?"

"London Swede just shot Oscar Olberg," was the answer.

"Shot him? Is he dead?" I asked.

"No, he isn't dead, but he will be dead." And somebody told how it happened.

Dutch Uncle, London Swede, Oscar Olberg and maybe others were drinking on London Swede's boat. Dutch Uncle was always a troublemaker. He started a rumpus between London Swede and Oscar Olberg. The quarrel continued, and London Swede got his gun. Oscar ran out on the deck with London Swede after him. Dutch Uncle dove overboard and swam ashore, underwater half the way.

Because the boat was lashed against piling, when London Swede shot Oscar, Oscar fell down in a heap against the piling.

Somebody called Dr. Kirby.

Somebody said, "Pack Oscar."

Oscar said, "No one's going to pack me."

Dr. Kirby said, "Don't pack him. Let him walk. He's shot through the heart, but let him walk till he drops."

However, they did pack him to Dr. Kirby's. They laid him there on the examining table. He didn't die, and he didn't die the next day or the third day.

The mailboat, the old Prince of Wales, came. Dr. Kirby had someone lug Oscar to the boat. They went to Ketchikan to Doc Ellis. Doc Ellis examined him and said, "The bullet has gone right through and has come out and apparently didn't hurt too much."

Dr. Kirby said, "The bullet didn't come out. The shirt had a hole in the front. There was a hole in his chest. There was a hole in his back, and the blood poured out the back, but there was no hole in the back of the man's shirt. We didn't find a bullet anywhere."

Doc Ellis said, "No hole in his shirt and no bullet, but the hole in his chest? A puzzle."

When Dr. Kirby got back from Ketchikan, he learned the answer to the mystery of the hole in Oscar but no hole in the shirt. One day Mrs. Kirby was cleaning. She said to Dr. Kirby, "You and your dirty socks," and she pitched one at him. A bullet rolled out. It was Oscar's sock. His black winter underwear was so stiff it had stopped the bullet, and the bullet rolled down into his sock.

Oscar wouldn't sign a complaint against London Swede, but London Swede was given six months for carelessly handling a gun.

John Landerman

This was around 1915-16, when Richard Hardcastle was mild-curing king salmon in Steamboat Bay on the north coast of Noyes Island. He had a pile-driver partner, a trapman from Puget Sound, this John Landerman.

John stuttered, and he spun yarns on himself. When he ridiculed himself, it sure was good material to repeat.

Hardcastle and Landerman planned to replace their mild-cure station at Steamboat Bay with a larger building. John went to Craig in his boat the Pauline B. to get some lumber. He headed up through shallow Portillo Channel, what we all called the "Cabbage Patch" because it had lots of kelp. In those days it was used only with local knowledge.

Along came a strange boat from below, that is from the Lower 48, with the captain headed for Noyes Island's prominent fishing grounds. He ran out on deck and waved his hat. John slowed his boat, took it out of gear and asked the cheechako what he wanted. The fellow said, "I want to know where is Noyes Island and how to get there."

John said, "W-w-well, just keep on g-g-going, because you'd b-b-be there long before I c-c-could tell you."

John put his boat in gear and took off for Craig.

⚞ ⚞ ⚞

John had married a widow, the mother of a 14-year-old boy. She taught school in Craig and later in Ketchikan.

The kid was working with John, building a floating fish trap. Because times were tough, John didn't have many tools to work with. The boy was driving the big trap staples with an old-type maul or sledgehammer and was missing the staples all the time. He broke the handle off the hammer. John ran over to him. "I don't see how such a l-l-lovely woman as your mother c-c-could ever have given b-b-birth to such a worthless k-k-kid as you," he said.

The young man had never spoken back to his stepdad. This

time he did. "That's what I always wondered—how a wonderful nice woman like my mother married a dirty old misfit like you."

John threw the big hammer the boy had been using overboard and put his arms around the youngster and said, "Son. You and I are just two l-l-lucky people. That's all it c-c-could be. We're just l-l-lucky."

The Hot Tub

We never forgot the handtroller with arthritis who built himself a hot tub at Hole-in-the-Wall. Hole-in-the-Wall is an anchorage for small boats on Esquibel Island, a handtrolling camp across from Steamboat Bay.

Somebody told this chap that baths in hot salt water were good for the aches and pains of his arthritis.

He built a brick framework around and over a firepit. He cut the end off a 50-gallon oil drum and rinsed and rinsed the drum. Then he set the drum on the bricks and filled the drum with salt water.

He made a good fire of driftwood under the drum. When he thought the fire had burned down and the hot coals would keep the drum heating, he climbed carefully into the bath. The water kept getting hotter and hotter. He found the drum's sharp edges too high to step over. Because of his arthritis and age, he couldn't lift himself up. The only thing he could do was to rock and rock until he capsized the tub. He just about boiled himself.

George James

Dan Starkweather told me about being at a trial at which George James gave a remarkable performance.

Fish and Wildlife employees had arrested three Petersburg fellows on the Phoenix for illegally fishing herring on the spawning grounds at Fish Egg Island. The prosecutor had three witnesses, and George James was one of them.

George James, when he was called on, with chalk on the

blackboard drew the whole scene of the activity at the herring spawning grounds. He even drew a picture of the skipper.

Old Jim Brown, the magistrate, stood there and looked at the likeness and said, "Well, I guess that's the way it was done, all right. You fellows are guilty."

Lots of those people in the early days were gifted. They could watch anything being done and then go do it themselves. Charley Demmert not only built boats but lengthened them later on. George James watched an upholsterer and went home and covered his own chair.

Remember John Barrymore, Movie Idol in the 1920s

One time when my daughter Jean was a baby, Nettie had appendicitis. We went to Wrangell, and I stayed at the Grant Hotel. Old Johnny Grant was a storyteller. He told me about a man who wanted to go fishing and hunting. He went halfway up the Stikine and didn't see any game. Afterward, in the lobby of the hotel, he complained, "I thought if you came to Alaska you could shoot deer or other animals without all the misery of going up the Stikine. I saw a lot of advertisement that was for nothing."

Johnny Grant told him, "Well, if you want to shoot deer and duck, I'll fix you up."

Johnny sent the man out with Darby Choquette. They took an outboard and ran up to the beach at Rocky Pass. They shot bear at the mouth of the creek and also all the ducks the man wanted.

He was well pleased. He was a friend of John Barrymore's, so when John Barrymore got his yacht the Enfanta, he found Darby Choquette to take him around these waters.

Barrymore dressed rough and mixed with people. Carolyn remembered his coming into Tongass Trading Co. and going to the basement where they kept the cheeses in the 1920s. He was a short little fellow and not good-looking. Going downstairs, he'd pat the clerk on the butt. Dolores Costello and their two little children used to come into Tongass Trading all the time.

In the '60s and maybe before, downtown store people were used to John Wayne's yearly visit. He always moored his sailboat at City Float.

A Bit of History

When I was born, people were ordering from Montgomery Ward in Portland. When Rose Inlet Cannery was built, from what I've heard, a fellow came up there as timekeeper or bookkeeper. He stayed about a month and left. That fall everybody around that part of the country got a Sears, Roebuck catalog. Right away people started sending to Sears in Seattle because that was closer than Portland, and the steamers by then ran more regular from Seattle. There was another mail order outfit, the National Cloak and Suit Co. of New York or something like that.

Trouble at Rose Inlet

The cannery at Rose Inlet started in about 1910. To build it, the owner towed an old sailing ship from San Francisco with everything aboard needed for construction. Emil Larson was superintendent, and he had a son named Alf. The tender Alf was named after him.

Women and Chinese men worked at Rose Inlet. The women had houses for the season and were paid a set amount per case of fish.

On this occasion, the women were out berry-picking and found a body on the beach. It was a Korean who had been missing. He had a piece of twine around his neck and two or three bullet holes in him. Some knife slashes, too.

Charley Sulzer from Hetta Inlet was the U.S. commissioner. Pete Sharp went after Sulzer, who came and ordered an investigation.

The place was searched, and evidence turned up to arrest one of the men. Sulzer ordered a jury picked. The fellow was found guilty and sent to a federal prison down south.

There was lots of violence at Rose Inlet. The Chinese contractor hired the men in San Francisco or Seattle. He brought them up. He sold them everything they wore, their food and their to-

83

bacco. You see, the cannery paid the boss, the contractor, and he paid the men. He also ran a gambling game at the cannery.

A friend of mine saw one of the employees shoot his boss and nephew right outside the bunkhouse. The worker had lost all his money gambling.

About five years ago, the man who had served the longest consecutive time for murder was released from a federal prison. He'd served 67 years. He'd been convicted at Rose Inlet Cannery.

Cans

I started working at Rose Inlet when I was 12, in 1916. I earned 50 cents a day, running a clinching machine that put the tops on cans and crimped them. One day a cap got caught. I reached out and cut my hand. The end of my finger was hanging on by a little bit of skin. The foreman rushed over, took the end, shoved the piece back on and tied it up tight. The end grew back on.

The history about the cans is interesting. First, sheets of raw tin were shipped up from San Francisco or Seattle. From that, workers cut out the cans, rolled them and soldered them by a machine operated by coal and later by kerosene. It looked like a bench with a furnace underneath. Later on, flattened "sanitary" cans already made were shipped up.

After the cans were filled, the lids were soldered on. The old-style fish can had two soldered holes, one to let the steam and gas escape when the can was passing through the soldering machine to have the lid soldered on and the other to vent the cans after the first cooking.

Women workers hand-packed each can. The Chinese men had cut the fish by hand with a big gang-type knife—hand-butchered the fish—and cut them the length of the can. The "iron chink," as it was called, even in the industry's ads, later eliminated the need for hand-butchering, cleaning and trimming the fish.

After the cans were filled, the lids were soldered on and holes were left in the lid. When the fish was cooked, the workers put a drop of solder on the hole. After the last hole was soldered, the workers tapped every can on the lid with a little mallet. If the can had a solid sound, it was all right. If it had a hollow sound, it wasn't sealed.

Nowadays the vacuum machine is an entirely different and faster process.

A Trapman's Viewpoint
Or, A Little About Traps

The season was six to seven weeks, plus a week or two to bring the traps out from the web stations, to set them up, anchor them and set the wire from the trap to the shore. Anchoring the traps was a careful and dangerous procedure. Every so often, the big roll of cable that unwound after the five-ton anchor was cut loose caught and killed one of the crew.

The watchman lived on the trap all season in an 8 × 10-foot shack. The toilet was outside. A rowboat sat on the skiff slide for transportation to shore for drinking water, bathing in the creek, collecting wood for the fire and bringing food from the cache. On the trap itself, the watchman had a box in the back to keep his food cool and a slab of bacon in front. He hung beer bottles into the water on a line.

Chicken wire held down by rocks, from the shore to the trap, prevented salmon bypassing the nets.

The first traps were pile traps. They were stationary, built on pilings driven into the bottom of bays. I remember coming around Cape Chacon once in 1924, seeing puffs of smoke every few miles from the pile-drivers.

James Heckman, superintendent at Loring in about 1910, perfected the first floating traps. They started in common use in Alaska about 1917.

Lydia Charles from Kasaan was one of Heckman's interpreters. Jones Yeltatzie's dad worked with Heckman, too. Lydia Charles told this.

It was illegal to fish the traps on Sundays, but the canneryman and trap watchmen found a way to do it. A rope that could open and close an apron was extended into the trap shack. If a plane dropped over the hill into the middle of the trap to look the situation over, the rope could be pulled, the apron lowered and the way opened for the fish to bypass the rest of the trap and go on out into the open water. The apron was supposed to be lowered on Sundays when there was no legal fishing.

A friend of mine, Owen Hunt, was on a trap during his college years. The watchman with him, Joe, heard a plane. Instead of staying inside, he ran outside the shack to pull the rope and fell through the planks. When the airplane zoomed down, the pilot saw the trap in order and Joe taking a swim.

Λ Λ Λ

During the long hours, one of the watchmen's hobbies was to kill seals and eagles for the bounty—a $2 bounty on seals and a $1 eagle bounty. The men sent the bulb of the seal's nose and the leg of an eagle to the game department. I guess some sent in one leg to Canada and collected on that, too.

Λ Λ Λ

Owen told me there were moments one never forgets, like hearing his fellow watchman, Tommy, singing all the way across Clarence Strait, "When her hair has turned to silver." He came rowing, shooting at the smokestack and singing. The boss had sent rum for the diver who worked on the traps, and Tommy had drunk it.

Owen Hunt was on fish traps for Ward Cove Packing Co., Win Brindle's, from the time he was 15 till the Second World War, when he was 21. Dick and Amanda Anderson owned the trap and sold to Ward Cove. The trap was located north of Cholmondeley Sound on the east coast of Prince of Wales Island in Clarence Strait, about an hour's run by boat from Ward Cove.

This year, because there had been lots of trouble sometimes, three men were on the trap. This particular night, Tommy Little and Wally McGovern were sleeping inside the trap shack. Owen's

86

job was to stay awake all night outside. He set the alarm clock every 15 minutes ahead in case he'd go to sleep.

About two in the morning, he heard a faint chug-a-lug, chug-a-lug, and saw phosphorus in the water. He went in and wakened Tommy and Wally.

The plan was to shoot the spotlight when the seiner used it. The seiner would come up to the trap in the dark. One crew member would jump on the trap and hold the trap watchman while the others lifted and brailed the trap. When the seiner turned the spotlight on the watchman, he couldn't see a darn thing.

On this night, all three watchmen had guns. Wally wouldn't go outside, but Tommy and Owen lay down on the trap behind one of the logs. When the spotlight came on, it didn't blind them. Owen shot it out, and glass flew in every direction.

Owen and Tommy kept shooting, and the seiner pulled out with all the crew cussing.

Chapter VII. Mailboats

In SOUTHEAST Alaska, the mail was first carried by canoe, propelled by paddling or sailing. Joseph Skulka, Thomas Skulka's brother, hauled mail and passengers from Wrangell to Howkan in a Haida 10-fathom canoe, making a few stops on the way.

Later, Mr. James Young, the storekeeper at Howkan, had a steam launch, the Iris, built for carrying the mail.

Captain Forss on the Roughrider and the Teddy hauled mail around Cape Chacon to the mines in Hetta Inlet. Captain Hofstad on the steamer Ragnhild carried mail from Hadley on the east coast of Prince of Wales Island to the mines in Hetta Inlet.

Boats of my time were the Peasant and the America First, operated by Pegleg. The Forrester ran up Lynn Canal. The Dart and the Discoverer were two of the last on the west coast run.

Then there was the Prince of Wales. A day or two before Thanksgiving in 1928, she hit a rock outside Phillips Island, 25 miles northwest of Craig, and sank. The crew saved the mail and rowed into Craig, where I lived. Frank Sharp, the skipper, asked if I would take my boat the Delaware up as far as Port Alexander at Cape Ommaney, the southern tip of Baranof Island, and on up north to the herring stations.

Because the engine on the Delaware was in the shop being rebored, I couldn't. But I knew a fellow who would charter his boat if I'd run it, so I agreed. Because I had fished and worked out of Noyes Island Cannery for New England Fish Co. for years, I knew those waters. Noyes Island is on the Pacific Ocean west of Prince of Wales Island.

I made my first mail trip on that charter. Then Neil Transportation Co. put the Estabeth on the run. She was considered one of the finest in the country. Before she came to Neil Transportation, she had been on the Juneau-Hoonah run up Lynn Canal.

The skipper on the Estabeth was Dewey Stack, still a good friend of mine. He hadn't been on the west coast run and on north to Chatham Strait, so he asked me to work with him, which I did till spring and fishing season.

On this run, Dewey Stack was having his 30th birthday. We'd come up Chatham Strait and were headed up Frederick Sound and coming up on Turnabout Island. It was blowing 40 to 50 miles an hour, cold as the devil, and making ice. Dewey came up to man his watch. He said, "I'll tell you something, Gil, you could do for me for my birthday. You could go down and put some coal in the Arcola." We had Arcola heat with radiators just like a house heater, central heat, and the stove was in the foc's'le. I went down and I fired that thing up, and boy, smoke and fire were coming out of the stack. She was really getting hot.

I said, "Well, there you are, Cap."

Dewey said, "The way it looks on the stack, there should be heat, but I don't feel much." I went on to bed.

After a couple of hours, Dewey called me and said, "Heh, what in the heck went on down there? I don't have any heat at all. It's absolutely cold."

When the cook went to fix breakfast the next morning, we found out what was wrong. One of the water lines had busted, and we'd lost a lot of pressure. That whole trip we had no heat, and it was in the middle of the winter.

In Petersburg, Dewey went uptown and bought a kerosene heater. We put it in the pilot house. We did get the water line fixed so the cook could get water, but the Arcola was cracked. There was no heat from that outfit.

Coming back down into Tokeen early in the morning, gosh, it was cold. I was at the wheel. I put this new kerosene stove under the pilot house stool and Dewey's mackinaw coat over the top. I was warm as toast till Dewey came up and retrieved his coat.

⋀ ⋀ ⋀

One time we were going back around Cape Chacon, and we had a leak in the hull someplace. We were watching and bailing and making as good time as possible. Bert said, "Why don't you talk to Dewey and tell him you'll take us on a short cut through Eureka Pass inside Point Marsh instead of going clean around outside Barrier Islands?" Eureka Channel is narrow and dangerous, especially for large boats. The Estabeth was just under 65 feet. To navigate the pass, local knowledge was and is needed.

I told Dewey, and he said, "OK."

I took her, and we came down through Eureka Pass. It was just eight o'clock when we got a couple of hundred yards from the narrows. It was Dewey's watch then, and I said, "OK, Cap, it's your watch." I started out the door just as though I was really going. Dewey grabbed me by the neck and the seat of the pants and set me back in front of the wheel.

Dewey said, "You're going to steer for another half hour anyway." I did.

⋀ ⋀ ⋀

Another night in the Estabeth, we were coming across Chatham Strait between Admiralty Island and Baranof Island. We'd seen the peaks of Patterson Point, silhouetted rugged and high against the sky, and the lights at the herring station. We headed up Patterson Bay, making for the lights, and here came another snow squall. We ran about five minutes, and holy smokes, the Estabeth stopped. Captain Dewey said, "What the hell did we hit?"

I said, "It must have been the mountain. Nothing else it could be. We hit the whole of Baranof Island." The snow was thick, and the night was so black you couldn't see the foremast from the pilot house.

"Don't take the clutch out," said Captain Dewey. Finally we could see. It was ice. The ice had broken off 10 inches thick, and we'd plowed right into it and torn a bit of iron bark off the stern. The snow let up, and we could see lights again at the plant. We started blowing the whistle. The watchman came out over the ice about a mile and got the plant's mail. We took off. That tough boat made it.

In the meantime, Carl Foss, a local contractor, salvaged the Prince of Wales, and he and Jim Wick, another contractor in Ketchikan, rebuilt her and tried her. Neil Transportation, however, was so badly hurt it folded. At that time, Jim Davis, who'd owned the Estabeth in Juneau, took her back, and he had her on the run for a good many years. During World War II, she burned.

The Venus and the Neptune

After Ed Williams with the Chacon and Bill Noyes with the Windsor (and the old Fairbanks), Bill Mueller, a halibut fisherman, went on the mail run with his little rebuilt schooners the Venus and the Neptune. In the 1940s, I hired on as engineer on the Venus with David Frank, a fellow from Hydaburg, as skipper. Bill Mueller's wife, Cora, was cook, and a friend of mine, Paul Paulson, was deckhand.

One night in March, we left Ketchikan on the Venus with a

few passengers and a load of freight for Port Alexander. It was blowing, but not too bad. About the time we got to Lincoln Rock, the wind was starting to kick up, and by the time we got to Snow Passage, which is normally rough, it was really foul.

A little before eight in the morning, Mark Lewis, a passenger, who later on had the fish-buying station at Point Baker, got up. "Well," he said. "Now weather like this! Suppose something would happen. What would a person do?"

"Well," I said, "something happens sometimes, and sometimes it goes for years and nothing happens. You figure what you'll do when the time comes."

My watch was over, and I called the skipper, Dave.

Dave said, "You'd better tell Cora to get the coffee going. When we get past these islands, it's going to be rough again."

I said, "Yeah."

I went to the galley to oil the engine. Everything looked all right. Cora was already making coffee.

When I came up, I said to Dave, "The coffee's about ready. Go. Have some."

Dave left. I was at the helm. Suddenly I saw smoke coming out of the ventilator by the engine room. I called to Dave, "Come here a minute. Take the wheel. Something's wrong."

I went down to the engine room. The electrical panel evidently had shorted out, because the whole panel was afire. I used the extinguisher and got the fire out on the switchboard. However, it had burned the wire in behind those tanks. Dave and I called Paul, and he got the other old-time fire extinguisher. As he was passing it down the companionway, the hose broke off. It discharged the whole thing on the engines instead of on any of the fire. By that time she was blazing good. Dave said he was going to run her ashore if he could find a shallow beach.

We ran past Point Macnamara, on the northwest shore of Zarembo Island. The flames were coming out of the back of the pilot house, and everybody was on the bow. When we were bucking the wind, the flames were going aft instead of to the bow, so we

92

were all right. We got in behind those rocks past Point Macnamara, and Dave ran her ashore full speed.

It was a sandy beach. All but Paul and I jumped and waded on in. Paul and I filled the lifeboat with some grub, blankets, tarps and the gun. We lowered the skiff on its davit lines, and as it was going down, because the ship was listing real bad, the lifeboat banged against the side of the hull, rupturing some of the seams.

We jumped into the lifeboat and had to bail as fast as we could to keep her afloat until we reached the land. Snow was on the ground, but it wasn't too cold. All we could do was to sit and watch the Venus burn.

She had started to burn about nine in the morning, and she burned till midnight, everything but the keel. The hold had been half-full of oil for Port Alexander, and that made a good fire.

To signal for help, we fired a few shots. A cannery tender going north at three knots never stopped.

We cut down some small hemlocks and with the boughs made kind of a lean-to and covered it in part with canvas.

We stayed that night on the beach with a big bonfire. The next morning, we fixed the lifeboat where the rivets had busted open. Then we cut some brush and took a piece of canvas and covered the beacon at Point Macnamara, so any boat coming through would investigate.

Dave, Paul and I rowed across Snow Pass to Point Colpoys, the northeast point of Prince of Wales Island, and on to the logging camp at Red Bay. Old Owens gave us something to eat and said he'd tow us back to pick up the people to take them to Wrangell. He started to tow us back with his camp tender the Josephine. We had just got past Point Colpoys and here came the Coast Guard power scow the Thistle. The crew had noticed the beacon covered, so they stopped to pick up the passengers and the cook. Dave, Paul and I got on board, and the Coast Guard took the lifeboat in tow. They took us all to Petersburg.

Casey Moran was the captain of the Thistle. After he left the Coast Guard, he started the Alaska Coast Pilot organization. He

93

was born in Alaska and was a real Alaskan.

We got to Petersburg. None of us had any money, and Cora fired us all. Although her husband owned the company, Cora was really the boss. The man in the hotel at Petersburg was pretty good and let us sleep in the lobby. That evening I ran into a fellow, Elwood Thomas, who used to fish with me when he was a kid. He took Dave, Paul and me out and bought us a couple or three beers. The next day, a Ketchikan contractor, Odin Jensen, a fine old man who had had a job there in Petersburg, ran into us. "My God," he said, "you boys got no money?" He gave us all $10 apiece.

He said, "Here, here, take it."

We said, "We can't."

But we did. A few days later, the Neptune came. Although Cora had fired us, we were rehired and shipped out on the Neptune. Two of her crew had quit. People were always quitting on those mailboats. There was lots of running and lots of freight to handle. In the wintertime, it was miserable.

Jim Pitcher

Jim Pitcher used to run mailboats from Ketchikan to Hyder. This is a run through Revillagigedo Channel, up Pearse Canal to Portland Canal, the boundary between the U.S. and Canada. Hyder is at the north of the canal, at the mouth of the Salmon River.

Jim worked for Noyes Transportation, which had the old Taku II. Fred McKay, Gene McKay's father, had it afterward. Gene now has tugboats in Ketchikan. Anyway, Jim was quite a character, an old-time prospector from Nome's early days. I knew him before he was on the Hyder run, when he was purser on the Estabeth. He had a good deal. He rode the Estabeth, doing purser work for the privilege of buying fur on his own.

On one stop at Klawock, Jim left his stinky favorite pipe in the post office. On his return back from Wrangell, the postmaster said, "A lady here found your pipe."

Jim said, "Oh my gosh, did she?"

"Yup."

"Who was she?"

The postmaster said, "That little old lady sitting right over there," and pointed to a bright-eyed, 75- or 80-year-old bashful lady.

Jim went over and threw his arms around her and kissed her right square on the lips.

This Jim was quite a talker. One night, the Estabeth went into the cannery and Native village at Karheen on the Wrangell run to Klawock. Jim bought some fur from the winter watchman. We were all talking a lot and finally came aboard, but Jim didn't. He had got halfway down the dock ladder and was hanging there still talking, the last anyone noticed. We all thought he was aboard. The skipper said, "OK, let the line go."

We ran clean up to Peep Rock, seven-tenths of a mile northwest of Karheen Cove.

Paul suddenly said, "Where's Jim?" He wasn't aboard, and we ran back. He and the winter watchman were up on the dock. Jim was watching for us. He knew we'd be back.

The End of the Mailboats

The airplane put a stop to the mailboats. When Bob Ellis started with his airplane, flying out to Craig from Ketchikan, he hauled the first-class mail and passengers. After World War II, he began his route to Craig and Klawock with a little plane. On the west coast, he'd take orders for groceries and all kinds of things. Then he'd fly back to Ketchikan, ride his bicycle around the old dirt and brick streets, fill the orders and then go back to the west coast with the cargo. His business grew until he had flights to any spot in Southeast, including Juneau, Skagway, the logging camps, the west coast towns and the airfield on Annette. His Grumman Geese met all the flights from Seattle and the north.

Anyway, the mailboats lost their first-class mail. Just about the only passengers for the boats were the ones in the wintertime going "Outside"—to the Lower 48. They took the boat when the weather was bad to ensure they made connections with the flights south.

Here's one of Bill Mueller's stories of those early airplane days: One time, just before Christmas and shortly before the Venus burned, Bill Mueller ran her into Craig. Bob Ellis and his plane had been stormbound there for two days. He had Christmas presents aboard for Ketchikan people and for mailing south.

Bob Ellis came down to the Venus. He said, "Bill, the weather's so bad I don't think I'll make it back to Ketchikan to take this stuff in by Christmas. Will you take it?"

Bill, with his German accent and waving his left hand, said, "Sure, Bob. And if you can get that damn plane on deck and fold the wings, we'll take that, too."

A Bit About Fox Ranches
and Herring Reduction Plants

The early mailboats stopped at the fox ranches and the herring reduction plants.

The first fox ranch I ever knew was on Strait Island, owned by the Clary brothers. I guess they made good, because they sold everything, breeders and pairs. Bob Race's father had a fox ranch up at Square Island. Square Island is near the entrance of Spacious Bay about 22 miles above Caamano Point on the west shore of Behm Canal.

Ray Peterson had a fox ranch over on Patterson Island, south of Kasaan Bay. And on Grindall Island, a woman had one. Clyde Cowan, who had the Amak, had one down at Carroll Inlet someplace.

Herring reduction plants took the oil out of the herring for use and ground the remnants for meal and fertilizer. They were called stink plants.

Chapter VIII. Loggers

Pike pole slim was a logger who had gotten his nickname from being a boom man for the Juneau Spruce Logging Co. He had a wife, Rosie, who's probably still living up around Juneau. He liked to tell about the first night he met her.

Pike Pole Slim had a home at Cape Pole on the western shore of Kosciusko Island and a shack or cabin at Edna Bay on the eastern shore. A Forest Service road ran across the island, connecting the shores.

One night, the skipper, Louie, brought the tug the Lumberman to Edna Bay to pick up a log raft. He tied up to the standing boom —logs chained together that formed a walkway to the shore. With Louie was Rosie, who was kind of his girlfriend as well as his cook.

Pike Pole Slim had been to Craig and had gotten whiskey there. He always liked to have plenty of whiskey around in case anything happened, like mosquito bites.

He invited Louie and Rosie to his cabin for a drink.

To get to land from the boat, they had to walk a hundred yards or so on boom sticks, which are logs toggled together with boom chains six or eight feet long. Pike Pole took Rosie by the hand and helped her over from the first log to the second. Then he lengthened out the boom chain holding the two logs together.

In a few minutes Louie came along. He took one look at the distance between the logs and turned back to his boat to wait there for Pike Pole and Rosie to return. Pike Pole always said that Louie, a great big man, was quite clumsy, and Pike Pole had been pretty sure he wouldn't try to jump over the cold water between the logs.

Pike Pole Slim and Rosie went to his shack, and two friends of his were there drinking, Unuk River Slim and Smokey Frankfurter.

They all sat around. Pike Pole Slim was getting tired of the company. He figured Rosie was the woman for him. He was going to propose to her soon as the right minute came.

He had a big caliber rifle, the real thing. As Pike Pole told it, everybody was talking and never noticed that he reached behind him, took his .348, aimed it right into the gravel floor and pulled the trigger.

He'd finish the story: "When the smoke cleared away, Rosie and I were alone, and we've been alone ever since."

Pike Pole Slim liked to tell about the long winter he was trapping at Whale Head Island. I don't know how he knew, but he was sure only he and one wolf were predators on the island and only one of them was going to survive.

He built a lean-to shelter of bark and hemlock boughs over his tent to keep the snow off. That took care of his housing. Now he had to think about his grub. He hadn't brought much. He had potatoes, flour and coffee, and he was relying on the hunting to supplement that. He looked around and found three beach feeder ducks, one Sitka black-tailed deer, sign of a few rock ptarmigan, butter clams on the beach and sign of a wolf.

First he went into the woods and shot the deer. He got back to camp and hung the meat high up to dry. It was already a cold winter. He got the ducks and prepared them. Then the ptarmigan. The wolf couldn't dig clams, so Pike Pole didn't have to dig those ahead of time.

Then he finished his story: "You know, in a month's time, the wolf came right to my door and gave up; so I shot him and got the skin."

Pike Pole always liked to get the best of anybody. This time he was teasing Jeff Anderson, a friend of his, who was bartending at the Alaska Bar. We were sitting close by Jeff, who was pouring drinks. He not only worked there but also was a guide for hunting parties.

Pike Pole said, "Jeff thinks he's a guide, and he's always telling stories. I'll tell you one that happened to me last spring."

Jeff was listening.

Pike Pole said he and a fellow by the name of Pearl Newell used to trap beaver together. One spring they went up Trout Creek looking for beaver sign. Pearl was going one way and Pike Pole another.

Pike Pole came to an open muskeg area. He looked around. In the middle of the muskeg was one lone bull pine. This was odd. For half a mile around, there were no other trees.

Pretty soon he heard a wolf howling. He said to himself, "Here comes a wolf." He heard another one howl, and all of a sudden seven of them were in the clearing.

Pike Pole didn't have his gun. Pearl, his partner, had taken it. Pike Pole had the hatchet to blaze the trail for beaver scent.

He climbed the bull pine. The wolves all around the tree couldn't get him, but it was cold sitting in the tree.

Pike Pole continued his story: "Now the wolves didn't howl or anything. With their mouths open, they just sat there looking at me. Finally they grouped together and had a powwow, yipping and yowling. Six of them took off. They left an old female. She looked at me, and I looked at her. Her teeth were pretty well gone. I thought, 'It's now or never. This wolf can't hurt me.'

"I loosened up the hatchet, got it in my hand and was ready to spring down to hit her with it. Then I was going to run for the beach.

"All of a sudden, I never heard such a noise in all my life. Here came the six wolves, howling and driving a beaver ahead of them, a beaver to cut the tree down!"

Jeff heard the whole story. He slammed down the bottle and the glasses he held. He said, "Pike Pole, get the heck out of here, you miserable so-and-so, and stay out."

100

Chapter IX. Russian Bob

Russian bob lived in Klawock. He was one everybody listened to. No matter what kind of trouble, no matter where, when he got up to make a speech, everybody quieted like at church and listened.

As elder in the Presbyterian Church, he held the people together. The Haida and the Tlingit had great respect for anybody with good sense. Proven good sense and calm dignity commanded faith.

Russian Bob [David Roberts] was the father-in-law of Bob (R.J.) Peratrovich, who owned the big store on Klawock's waterfront. Russian Bob's big blue eyes, long white beard and white moustache gave credibility to the stories that he was part Russian.

This was a long time ago, when George Hamilton's first wife died in Craig. Four or five of us, including Jim Edenso, Eddie Cogo and me, who all had lived in Howkan as had George Hamilton, went by boat to Bob Peratrovich's store to bring the coffin to Craig. We tied up at R.J.'s 60-foot dock and went into the store to arrange to get the casket. Bob Peratrovich said he'd have the coffin taken to the boat. "While I'm doing that, you go next door to my father-in-law's. He wants you to come to his home for tea and cake."

We went next door, and Russian Bob met us. We went into the living room and sat down. The wife stayed in the kitchen, which was customary in those days. Some of the nieces brought out the cake and tea to serve us.

We all sat quietly for a while. Russian Bob was the one who had asked us there, so no one else started any conversation. We were comfortable with waiting for the host. This was our way.

Then, so everybody could understand, Russian Bob said in Chinook:

"Life is a funny thing. It's a wonderful thing. It's good. How-

101

ever, when you have your heart full of sorrow, you walk down the street and it seems there are thousands of people. You look at them. You wonder what they are thinking about. Maybe they have as much sadness or more in their hearts. You don't know because you don't know them.

"We can never understand death, especially when a man loses his wife. It's like the man's all alone way out in the ocean, huddled on a rock. He doesn't know what to do. He doesn't know which way to look. He's cold. It's foggy. He can't see far. He doesn't know where he is.

"But as time goes on, he looks. The water's going down around the rock. Then he can see land, and pretty soon the rock becomes part of the land. He can walk ashore.

"People are there. It's a new life. It's not the same as it was before the flood, but he has to learn to live with it."

Russian Bob said a prayer in Tlingit and that was the end.

Totems and graves, Howkan, 1897 (Winter & Pond, courtesy of Alaska
Historical Library, 87-58)

References

The following works were useful in preparing the Introduction to *Gilbert Said*:

Books:

Alaska, Its Southern Coast and the Sitkan Archipelago, by Ruhannah E. Scidmore (D. Lothrop and Co., 32 Franklin St., Boston, 1885). From pp. 269-279:

> . . . It was a wet and gloomy afternoon when the Idaho anchored in the little American Bay on Dall Island, not more than a mile from Howkan, an ancient settlement of the Kaigahnee Haidas and a place of note in the archipelago. Howkan has more totem poles than any other village, and is one of the most interesting places on the route. . . . The fur traders used always to anchor in the little bays on the opposite shore, and to one of them, American Bay, the Northwest Trading Co. was about to move its stores.
>
> . . . The missionaries named (Howkan) "Jackson" in honor of the Rev. Sheldon Jackson, the projector and manager of Presbyterian missions in Alaska, and the Post Office Department recognized it as "Haida Mission" when the blanks and cancelling stamps were sent out for the small post-office. . . . A request was made by the mission people to have the place put down as Jackson on the new charts, since issued by the Coast Survey, but the commander of the surveying steamer opposed it as an act of vandalism, and on the maps it still retains the . . . old . . . name.
>
> . . . Skolka has a large house guarded by two totem poles, and at his offer the house had been occupied for two years as a school-room by the mission teacher. A flagstaff and a skeleton bell-tower were added to the exterior decorations of his house.

Indians of the Northwest Coast, by Philip Drucker (American Museum Science Books, published for the American Museum of Natural History, The Natural History Press, Garden City, N.Y., 1955). From p. 12: "It is said that the Alaskan Haida, known as the Kaigani, drove out some Southern Tlingit tribe or tribes a little more than two centuries ago."

The Mushing Parson, by Stanley Hall Young (Fleming H. Revell Co., New York and Chicago, MCMXXVII).

105

The Silver Years of the Alaska Canned Salmon Industry, edited by Laurence Freeburn (Alaska Northwest Publishing Co., 1976).

Reports:

Among the Alaskans, by Julia McNair Wright for the Presbyterian Board of Publications, 1883, contains a chronology of events in Alaska missions, 1877-1883, from which the following is extracted:

Aug. 10, 1877. The Rev. Sheldon Jackson and Mrs. A.R. McFarland land at Fort Wrangell and commence Presbyterian missions in Alaska.

Aug. 8, 1878. The Rev. S.H. Young arrives at Fort Wrangell.

Aug. 12, 1879. Dr. Jackson starts on a canoe trip of 250 miles and holds councils with the chiefs of the Hydah, Tongass, Tsimpshean and Chilcat tribes.

April 1880. The Revs. S.H. Young and G.W. Lyon make a canoe trip among the Hydah villages.

Aug. 22, 1881. Drs. Corlies and Jackson and Mr. J.E. Chapman set out on a canoe trip of 500 miles (round trip) to the Hydah villages on Prince of Wales Island. A mission, named by the missionaries "Jackson," located near the Indian village of Howkan.

Sept. 12, 1881. Mr. Chapman opens the mission school at Jackson. ("Skule-ka gave the best house in his village, he a leading chief of the Hydahs, for a school and his wife does the teacher's washing free of charge . . . saying he was teaching them freely and she would wash for him in like manner," wrote Dr. Jackson later.)

Feb. 4, 1882. Post office secured by Dr. Jackson for Roberts, on Fontaine Bay, Klawock, Jackson and Haines.

May 1882. The Rev. J.L. Gould reaches Jackson.

Sept. 10, 1882. Sawmill, purchased with funds raised by Dr. Jackson and Mrs. J.M. Ham, is landed at Jackson. Miss C.A. Gould, missionary-teacher, reaches Jackson.

March 1883. Dr. Jackson receives a contract from the U.S. Post Office Department to supply the stations at Haines, Roberts, Klawock and Jackson with a monthly mail, to be carried by Indians in canoes.

June 1883. Mr. W. Donald McLeod is sent to Jackson to erect the sawmill and teach the Natives how to use it.

Report of the General Agent of Education in Alaska for the Year 1890-1891, by Sheldon Jackson, General Agent (U.S. Government Printing

Office, Washington, 1899).

Education in Alaska, 1892-93, by Sheldon Jackson, General Agent (U.S. Government Printing Office, Washington, 1895).

Education in Alaska, 1897-98, by Sheldon Jackson, General Agent (U.S. Government Printing Office, Washington, 1899).

Report on Population and Resources of Alaska at the Eleventh Census, 1890 (Census Office, Department of the Interior; U.S. Government Printing Office, Washington, 1893), beginning p. 31:

> Howkan (Jackson post office) is situated upon the west side of Long Island (which lies between the south end of Prince Edward Island and Dall Island), and next to Port Chester is the most important Native village in this part of the territory. . . .
>
> Rev. J. Loomis Gould, the Presbyterian missionary at this place, has been unremitting in his efforts with these people for the past 9 years, and has been ably seconded in his work by his wife, a woman of charming character, who possesses many of the charitable and philanthropic traits which have distinguished her sister, Mrs. McFarland, so long stationed at Fort Wrangell, but now in charge of the children's home here.
>
> There are but 2 white men living at the mission besides the missionary, one the superintendent of the sawmill and the other the storekeeper. This village is about 175 miles distant from Fort Wrangell by the usual route, and probably its remoteness from white settlements has aided in the success of the missionary work among these people.
>
> The public school here, supported by the general government, is presided over by a sister of Mr. Gould, and her work among the Native children has been marked by excellent results.
>
> The children's home, in charge of Mrs. McFarland, and supported by the Presbyterian Board of Home Missions, is occupying temporary quarters, the pretty buildings built for that purpose having been destroyed by fire a year ago. . . . Howkan has a post office called Jackson, and receives mail from Fort Wrangell once a month. The regular Alaska steamers make visits to this place only twice a year, once in the autumn and once in the spring, and remain only long enough to discharge their freight.
>
> The village of Howkan contains about 40 houses, among them a number of neat and pretty cottages occupied by Natives. At the

time of my visit most of the people were away for the summer, fishing and working at different canneries. There is an elaborate display of totems here, the carvings upon them being of the best workmanship. From my observations I am led to believe that the Haida rank second at least among all the other tribes in the practice of industrial pursuits, many of them displaying rare mechanical skill.

There is a general store here, which carries a stock of several thousand dollars and does a large business. Besides dealing with the resident Haida, many of those living on the Queen Charlotte Islands do more or less trading here, bringing their furs, which they exchange for goods.

About 20 miles south of Howkan is a place sometimes occupied by . . . Kaigani. It is at the southern point of Dall Island, which lies on the opposite side of Howkan Strait, a body of water a mile or so wide separating this island from Long Island. Between Kaigani and the Queen Charlotte Islands the Haida hunt sea otter, this channel being a resort for this most valuable of fur-bearing animals, though they are not very numerous. . . .

About 3 miles south of Howkan, on the opposite side of the strait, is located a sawmill which is run by water power. For the past 5 years it has been made to furnish lumber for the mission and also for the Natives. None of the lumber cut here has been sold to the white settlers or sent away from this immediate vicinity. The mill is run by Natives with the help of the superintendent, a part of whose duties it is to instruct them in the use of tools and in the various branches of labor. . . .

At the time of my visit to this place the weather was so bad I had to remain here 4 days. The next day after my arrival the steam launch from Taku arrived, bringing Mr. Miller and his wife and daughter. An idea of the remoteness of Jackson from other settlements, and the rare visits made by strangers, is best understood when I state that Mrs. Gould told me this was the first time during her residence of 9 years that she had had the pleasure of entertaining a white woman.

["Mr. Miller" would have been Mr. James Millar, father of Craig Millar. James Millar had a saltery near Klinquan at Hunter's Bay.

[Margaret E. Bell, granddaughter of James Millar, wrote autobiographical fiction for teenage girls. She describes life at Klinquan, near

Howkan, and mentions Howkan frequently in her books, *Watch for a Tall White Sail* (1948), *The Totem Casts a Shadow* (1949), and *Love is Forever* (1954), published by William Morrow and Co., New York. MLS]

French Creek Presbyterian Church, A Memorial to the 150 Years of Service of the French Creek Presbyterian Church, by Lois M. Pinnell (McClain Printing Co., Parsons, West Virginia, 36287, 1971) contains these references to the Rev. J. Loomis Gould:

> J. Loomis Gould became superintendent of the Upshur County schools in 1867. He designed the octagonal shaped building that housed the French Creek Institute. (p. 197)
>
> . . . he had visited his mother's people in the West and had seen such a building, which took his eye. The building was a source of worry to many people in the community, for they had the feeling that it might collapse from sheer weight of the roof. So, iron rods were installed by Professor Meigs. . . . (p. 206)

[The school in Howkan was octagonal and was designed by Loomis Gould. MLS]

Other materials:

The Alaskan, Sitka newspaper, Nov. 7, 1885; Feb. 20 and 27, 1886; March 6, 13 and 15, 1886; June 5, 1886; Jan. 18, 1887.

Dictionary of Alaska Place Names, by Donald J. Orth (Geological Survey Professional Paper #567, U.S. Government Printing Office, Washington, 1967).

The North Star, A Monthly Publication on Alaska Missions, December 1887 to December 1892, by Sheldon Jackson and Others. Sitka. Reproduced by The Shorey Book Store, Seattle, 1973.

The Polk Directory 1905-06, Alaska Yukon Gazetteer and Business Directory (R.L. Polk, Seattle), lists Jackson with a population of 250. From p. 204:

> A P.O. and Indian village also known as Howkan or Long Island, in Dixon Entrance, 90 miles SW of Ketchikan and 650 miles from Seattle, the nearest banking point. Shipments may be made via Wrangell, with which place it has steamer connection. Sustains a Presbyterian church and general store. Some mining properties are

worked in the vicinity. Mail weekly from Wrangell by steamer. J.L. Gould, PM; Gould, J.L., mining; Young Trading Co., General Mdse.

The community is also included in the directories for 1909-10 and 1911-12, under the name of Howkan. The names of Gould and Young are gone, and W.E. Ross is listed as General Mdse. and Postmaster.

The McLeod family records contain letters to Clara Gould about her teaching position:

August 4, 1886
Madame:
 I enclose with great pleasure your commission for another year. You will commence your school on Monday, September 6. The instructions and regulations of last year will be good this. You will send your monthly reports as usual in duplicate to this office in Washington. I hope to visit your school in September or October.
 Truly yours,
 Sheldon Jackson, General Agent

April 11, 1887
 Yours without date enclosing check is received.
 As to not having taught in August makes no difference with the bill. Last year being paid by the year you were entitled to so much during vacations the same as if you had taught. This year it will be different as you are paid by the month.
 I find upon examining the books that you were paid

Dec. 5, 1885	$123.87
April 16, 1886	216.80
June 30, 1886	150.00
August 16, 1886	83.11
	573.78
	− 600.00
	26.22

This leaves $26.22 still due you on 1885 and 1886. How it happened I cannot say. It is the result of the attempt to pay by the year which I can explain to you if you call it up when we meet.
 I will try and collect on the eleven days of August 1886 which if I succeed will give you $16 or $17.00. The remaining $10.00 I trust

you will be willing to forego in view of the fact that the Bureau increased your salary $200.00 this year without solicitation or expectation on your part.

If the above is not satisfactory please let me know and will pay you myself as I cannot get it for you from the government.

Until further notice address me at Sitka, Alaska. Also send reports to me there. For official communications to me, reports etc., you can use the Penalty envelope.

Truly yours,

Sheldon Jackson, General Agent

Recommended reading:

Reporter at Large, "The Uncommitted Crime," by Alec Wilkinson (*The New Yorker*, Nov. 26, 1990), tells of the destruction of Angoon, an Indian town on Admiralty Island, by the Navy in 1882, with a clear picture of the days of trading and lawlessness preceding the establishment of government in Alaska and a good description of present-day Angoon. The author talks of the Tlingit living successfully with the land for a thousand years whereas with the white man's coming it took only a hundred years to have trouble with the forests, game and fish. [A sidelight: The missionaries at Haines struggled unsuccessfully to stop the Chilkats from harvesting seasonal fish on Sundays. When the runs came in and it was imperative they harvest, the missionaries tried to stop them. The Chilkats eventually learned the lesson and then refused on Sundays to pack for the desperate miners going up the Chilkat trail. MLS]

Chapter I, Gilbert in 1969 Talked About the Haida:

Children of the Raven, by H.R. Hays (McGraw-Hill Book Co., New York, St. Louis, San Francisco, 1975).

Indian Life on the Northwest Coast of North America, by Erna Gunther (University of Chicago Press, Chicago and London, 1975).

Indians of the Northwest Coast, by Philip Drucker, *ibid*.

A Pour of Rain, Stories from a West Coast Fort, by Helen Young Meilleur (Sono Nis Press, Victoria, B.C., v8w2j8 1980).

The Queen Charlotte Islands, 1774-1966, by Kathleen E. Dalzell (C.M. Adem SSI, Terrace, B.C., 1968).

111

The Shipwreck of the State of California (Alaska State Historical Library, Alaska, 1990.0026) gives details of the sinking mentioned in "The Shaman/Carolyn's Story."

The Tlingit Indians, by Aurel Krause, translated by Erna Gunther (University of Washington Press, Seattle and London, fourth printing 1978).

"Ravens," by Dorcas MacClintock (*Pacific Discovery*, Vol. XXIV, June 1971).

A story of the double-finned whale is told in *Yahk'll* (student magazine published by the Ketchikan High School Indian Education Program, third edition): "A Story as Told by Verna Mason," by Charlene Sykes.

The Craig students in 1976 published a magazine titled *Kil-Kaas-Git*, which carries an interview with Robert Cogo, whose childhood home was Klinquan, the Indian village near the saltery at Hunter's Bay where James Millar started his saltery.

Cogo talks of all the Haida villages with their old Tlingit names in which Haida lived at the time he was young. He talked of the move to Craig and of the Tlingits having given the Craig area to the Haida in reparation of a wrong.

[I have the same feeling reading these magazines as I do listening to Gilbert McLeod's stories. He is more Alaskan than West Virginia Presbyterian. He and I know well he is not an Alaskan by blood, but he was born as was Robert Cogo in the Haida country. When a child is not sure who he is, it must be difficult. He and I sincerely hope that these stories as he remembered them and as I edited them offend no one. MLS]

Another account of the double-finned whale is given in "Al Brown's Corner" of the *New Alaskan*, August 1987 (since reprinted on other dates).

Chapter II, Big Daykoo:

From *The Alaskan* (Sitka, May 15, 1886):

> The Mail is just in from Howcan, and we learn that McLeod, the missionary saw-miller, had been over near Mesachie Nose ["bad nose"—Cape Chacon] and had found several

ledges of very rich ore, in fact he had a mountain of it, and had the whole Hydah tribe
watching it. From the specimen I saw in the
hands of one . . . I should think it would assay
as follows:
   Traces of gold—none
   Traces of silver—none
   Other valuable minerals—none
   Bait for suckers—poor
Fearing that there might be a great rush and
many disappointments, I would say that it is
now too late as the whole country has been
staked.

*The Boundary Hunters, Surveying the 141st Meridian, The Alaska
Panhandle,* by Lewis Green (University of British Columbia Press,
Vancouver and London, 1982).

History of Mines and Prospects, Ketchikan District prior to 1952, by
John Bufvers (Division of Mines and Minerals, Department of Natural
Resources, State of Alaska, February 1967).

The State of Alaska, by Ernest Gruening (Random House, New
York, 1968.1954), p. 360. In his address to Congress in January 1905,
President Theodore Roosevelt presented the report of Lieutenant
George T. Emmons, U.S. Navy (retired), on the needs of the Alaskans.
Emmons listed those needs as (1) definition of legal status to give
them equality before the law; (2) the right to file a mining claim;
(3) the right to take up land; (4) the right to get a mariner's license;
(5) extension of the educational system, including vocational training;
(6) hospitals and dispensaries. He also talked of the need for protection of the northern groups' basic food supplies.

Tlingit and Haida Appraisal, Southeastern Alaska, by C. Marc
Miller and Associates, Real Estate Appraisers, Seattle, March 1962.

Chapter V, Gilbert Remembers Sulzer:

Frontier Politics, Alaska's James Wickersham, by Evangeline Atwood
(Binford & Mort, Thomas Binford, Publishing, Portland, Ore., 97202,
1979):

Charles August Sulzer came to Alaska in 1902. He was elected to the territorial Senate two years before the battle with Wickersham. His brother William was a congressman for sixteen years in New York and later governor of New York. He visited Alaska often (pp. 307-320).

Sulzer died aboard his yacht the Taku II. (p. 326)

The State of Alaska, Gruening, *ibid.:* In 1916, Wickersham ran as a Republican for the 64th Congress against Charles Sulzer, a Democrat. "After an exceedingly bitter campaign the canvassing board established in 1906 . . . found Wickersham elected by 31 votes." The territorial attorney-general invalidated votes of some remote communities in which ballots had not been received on election day. Decision appealed. Judge Robert W. Jennings ruled in favor of Sulzer, to whom he granted a certificate of election. Wickersham contested, and the House of Representatives declared him elected, but not until the session of Congress had expired.

Both filed for the 65th Congress. The results of the election were close. Sulzer died April 16, 1919, before the count was announced. Two days after his death, he was declared the winner. Wickersham declared himself elected. Again he was seated by the House but only three days before the end of the session (p. 287).

Charles August Sulzer was the brother of William Sulzer, representative from New York and later governor of New York (p. 287).

Rep. W. Sulzer argued for territorial status for Alaska in the 54th Congress (p. 138).

Since 1906 Alaska had sent an elected delegate to Congress, a delegate who had no voting power and could speak to members of Congress only when asked (p. 139).

Only on June 2, 1924, did federal legislation give all Alaskans citizenship (p. 363).

"Rastus Brown":

"On the Beach: Saltwater Huck Finns," by Charles Lillard (*Times Colonist*, Islander, Victoria, B.C., Sunday, March 13, 1988). Lillard quotes Bonnycastle Dale in *Milne's Landing*, 1911: "They are the beachcombers, the water gypsies of the Pacific," and mentions Rastus Brown, a "7-foot Norseman."

Pacific Coastal Liners, by Gordon Newell and Joe Williamson (Superior Publishing Co., Seattle, 1959), tells of the Mariposa ("Bad luck caught her one foggy night") and has a picture of the Sea Wolf, "a tiny gas schooner."

Chapter VI, Fishermen:

Southeast Alaska's Panhandle, Alaska Geographic, by Patricia Roppel with editors Robert N. DeArmond, Robert A. Henning, Marty Loken, Lael Morgan, Barbara Olds (Alaska Northwest Publishing Co., Anchorage, 1978):

Mild curing, or light salting, began on Fish Egg Island in April 1907. Mentioned in an account of Craig Millar's cannery at Waterfall in 1912 (p. 68).

Tlingit and Haida Appraisal, Miller and Associates, *ibid.*

Travels in Alaska, by John Muir (Houghton-Mifflin Co., Boston, 1915) mentions Choquette's Landing (pp. 97-112).

Chapter VII, Mailboats:

The Alaskan, Jan. 15, 1887, published a story by Chincat about his passage on the trial voyage of the Iris, built for Mr. James Young to carry the mail between Fort Wrangell and Howkan, leaving Wrangell Oct. 27, 1886.

Among the Alaskans, by Wright, *ibid.*

A Pour of Rain, by Meilleur, *ibid.*, p. 269: "Later James Young's son had the Mabel, a 28-foot steamer and sloop for carrying mail and the 36-foot Tiding. The Tiding was sold in 1907."

From a letter to MLS from the Alaska State Historical Library:

(The Venus) burned early March 21, 1946, off Point Macnamara. Beached on Rookery Island. Owens of the logging camp in Red Bay came out and took crew and passengers to his camp. Burned to the water's edge with no loss of life. Capt. David Frank and Chief Gilbert McLeod were in her. She had been rebuilt from her original halibut schooner design to a double-decker aft and placed on the west coast mail run.

The maps and references in the *U.S. Coast Pilot, Southeast Alaska*, have been invaluable throughout the production of *Gilbert Said*. I have used primarily the Tenth (1952) Edition (U.S. Government Printing Office, Washington, D.C.), along with U.S. Geological Survey maps of southeastern Alaska. Where there are discrepancies, the map of Gilbert's world uses the most recent USGS spellings of place names.

Gilbert and Carolyn McLeod, beachcombing at McLeod Bay, 1982

By Maleta Boatman

M ARIAN L. SWAIN was born in Iowa in 1914. Since her University of Iowa days, she has been interested in different cultures. She has a master's degree in social work and received training at the University of Chicago and at Hull House—but if she had it to do again, she says, she would be a social anthropologist. She lived in Ketchikan, Alaska, on the island of Revillagigedo, from 1953 to 1977 and is the mother of two sons.

Gilbert Said is her first book. She is at work on the journals of her travels in a motor home with her sister throughout much of Canada and the United States—including Alaska—and of her life since 1977 in a beach cabin on an island in Washington state.

Gilbert Said

Book design and production: David R. Johnson
Editing and production: Jackie Pels
Maps and chapter illustrations by John Boring
Technical assistance: Werner Pels, Drew DeVigal and Jerry Telfer

McLeod family photos, except as noted
The portrait of Gilbert McLeod on the Ketchikan waterfront, p. 21, is a
reproduction of an oil painting by Michele McGill, his stepdaughter
The photo on p. 36 is of Gilbert McLeod and his sisters, Margaret
and Jean, in 1914
The 1910 view of Forrester Island, p. 48, is a Young family photo
lent by Helen Young Meilleur

Front cover photo of Howkan courtesy of Alaska Historical Library
(Winter & Pond, 87-91)
Back cover photo of Chief Skulka's totem courtesy of Alaska
Historical Library (Edward de Groff, 91-55)

Composition by Archetype Typography, Berkeley, California
Printed and bound at Inkworks, Berkeley, California
Alkaline pH recycled paper (Revue by Monadnock)

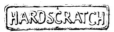

Hardscratch Press
2358 Banbury Place
Walnut Creek, CA 94598
510/935-3422